T0167095

Number Three in the "Created For" Series: Purpose

CREATED *for* PURPOSE

Answering the Common Question, "What Am I Here For?"

Robert B. Shaw, Jr.

WESTBOW
PRESS®
A DIVISION OF THOMAS NELSON
& ZONDERVAN

All Scripture references are from the New American Standard Version of the Bible, Holman Bible Publishers, 1981, unless otherwise noted.

The New International Version (NIV) of the Bible used is the NIV Study Bible, tenth anniversary edition, Zondervan Publishing House, Grand Rapids, Michigan, 1995.

The King James Version (KJV) of the Bible used is published by Hendrickson Publishers, Peabody, Massachusetts, 2006.

The New Living Translation (NLT) of the Bible used is the NLT Life Recovery Bible, published by Tyndale House Publishers, Carol Stream, Illinois, 1998.

WestBow Press books may be ordered through booksellers or by contacting:

WestBow Press
A Division of Thomas Nelson & Zondervan
1663 Liberty Drive
Bloomington, IN 47403
www.westbowpress.com
844-714-3454

ISBN: 978-1-4908-6405-1 (sc)
ISBN: 978-1-4908-6406-8 (hc)
ISBN: 978-1-4908-6441-9 (e)

Library of Congress Control Number: 2014922543

Print information available on the last page.

WestBow Press rev. date: 05/22/2024

Contents

Foreword

⌒⌒

T he news media often describes the events of the day in terms of our conflicts, confusion and chaos. Long ago someone observed that a meaningless universe becomes a mean one. The quest for meaning and purpose is as old as man. Dr. Shaw's book, *Created for Purpose*, makes a major contribution in bringing meaning, light and insight into the arena of human complexity. The age old question of who are we, how did we get here, why are we here and where are we headed are tackled with clarity and sophistication. Dr. Shaw addresses our core longings by going to the heart of life's most meaningful questions and without bumper sticker catch phrases or political correctness. Dr. Shaw utilizes his range of experience in education, psychology, sociology and theology to address life's issues of self-discovery, relationships, significance and fulfillment.

Men have attempted, through our finite understanding, to address how we came into being and the meaning of our existence. Varying views have emerged over time:

> ...we exist by random chance
> ...we are *victims* of inadequate parenting thus
> ...we are underdeveloped children
> ...we are only who we say we are
> ...we are by-products of socialization
> ...we are shaped *primarily* by our environment

Dr. Shaw departs from man's theories and utilizes rather the designer's manual. Buy an automobile, build a home, install a computer system or assemble your children's Christmas gifts and you find out quickly consulting the original architect, designer and his manual is essential. Created for Purpose will make a deposit of meaning, purpose, destiny and legacy to your understanding of who you are, what you are designed to do, and the world you live in. This book is an inspirational, insightful, instructional, and a must read for everyone seeking greater meaning and enduring fulfillment.

Finally, on a personal level, I have known Bob for more than twenty years as:

- As husband, father and grandfather to his family
- Administrator and minister
- Associate Pastor and Elder
- Clinician and Counselor
- Teacher and Professor
- Friend and Confidant

Today he is emerging as an important writer and author called to help each of us fulfill our God-given purpose and thus reach our best and highest self!

Rev. David A Longobardo
Pastor, Educator, International Speaker and Leader Developer for Over 35 Years;
A Pastor to Pastors
Currently, Pastor Emeritus
World Vision International Christian Center (WVICC)
Greensboro, North Carolina

Introduction

C ore longings are meant to draw us into God's embrace so that we can find rest and contentment. They were created by God to be met by God. I want to acknowledge Dr. Terry Wardle and Dr. Ann Halley of Ashland Theological Seminary for their teachings regarding core longings and for their ministries related to inner healing and formational counseling.

One of our core longings is the desire to know our purpose. These longings are universal, transcending age, gender, ethnic background, and culture. This book is the third in a series, *Created For*, which discusses the six core longings of every human being:

- significance
- safety (covering)
- purpose
- understanding
- belonging
- love

Peace and contentment occur when we feel our longings are being met. "When God created Adam and Eve He placed within them certain undeniable longings meant to be fulfilled in Him, with Him and through Him" (Wardle 2005, 64). When our core longings are not met, we usually try to meet them on our own. That is when we often get into trouble. "Underneath every problem there is always an unfulfilled desire" (Laaser 2008, 41).

Over the centuries, in most cultures, questions related to one's purpose were perhaps easier to answer than in our day and age. Early in human history, the family was the nurturing ground for launching young people into their purpose. A person's vocation and role in the community were often seen as givens and depended upon what the person's parents did, especially the father, or what the community needed at the time.

In most cases, a woman's choices were to be a mother, to work on a farm, to be a homemaker, a nurse, a seamstress, or a teacher. For men, the choices were factory worker, farmer, military warrior, construction worker, physician, salesman, business owner, or political leader. In other cultures, women performed child care, farming, and meal preparation. The men would be hunters, lumberjacks, warriors, tribal leaders, and workers who would build homes, temples, and gathering places for their communities. Because the choices were few, finding one's purpose was not difficult.

Today, the choices are seemingly endless, making the discovery of purpose more confusing and difficult. Or so it seems. But it is not only the countless choices that make finding our purpose tougher. The more we distance ourselves from God and His standards, the more we become confused, lost, and desperate. We can select from so much more of what the world offers. As a result, we often choose what is pragmatic but not fulfilling. We choose what will bring us the most income, which is indeed important, but at the expense of our passions and dreams—if we even know what those are.

More and more people live their lives for momentary pleasure rather than for sustained peace and contentment. People are seeking happiness when what they really want is peace and contentment.

Happiness is based upon circumstances that bring pleasure and, as such, come and go. Peace and contentment come from within and are developed through a sense of purpose and the fulfillment of that purpose.

The desire for purpose is manifested by the pursuit of happiness and by answering the question, "What am I here for?" or "What am I supposed to do with my life?" Someone who says, "I just want to be happy," is often seeking peace and contentment. Happiness is situational and fleeting, while peace and contentment are more about our core longings being satisfied and are more sustaining. We can experience peace and contentment when we know our longings are being met, and those longings include our purpose.

Our true sense of purpose begins with a relationship with God. This may sound simplistic, but the idea is profound and life-changing. The more we distance ourselves from God, the less we know ourselves and the more baffled we are. The less we seek relationship with God, the more we find ourselves without a direction in life. This is true of Christians as well. In fact, of all people on earth Christians should have the clearest picture of their destiny. Christians and non-Christians alike long to know their purpose, and it begins with declaring that Jesus is not only our Savior, but Lord of our life.

God is our creator, and as our creator, He knows what is best for us and what His plans are for us. To find our true purpose, all of us need to know God and to hear from Him what His intentions are. Admittedly, this is easier said than done much of the time. Hearing from God is one of the most, if not the most, challenging aspects of our Christian faith. Discovering what He expects of us is essentially a lifelong journey.

However, we *can* know God's specific purpose for our lives. We learn this ultimately through His Word. Most Christians today are primarily New Testament-oriented. As a result, we miss so much of God's story and of His desires for humanity. The New Testament builds upon what God said in the Old Testament and reveals more clearly His nature and His plan in the life, teachings, death, and resurrection of Jesus Christ. The Old Testament provides a framework for God's nature and our purpose as human beings. I am specifically referring to the first few chapters of Genesis and to a fresh look at the Ten Commandments.

The Ten Commandments are more than just the beginning of the Law. They provide a revealing sense for our purpose, as God has designed it for us. Our purpose is two fold: to glorify God and be a blessing to our fellow man. There are many ways these two dynamics are manifested, which will be spelled out in this book. The commandments spawn the many ways of life that can develop into our purpose. It is not by accident that we have lost our way and struggle with our purpose in life as we have distanced ourselves from the commandments that God used to establish His ways for His people. My prayer is that this series, and this book, will help position us for a discovery of that purpose.

Our loving heavenly Father desires to reveal what He has in store for us. He is a God who gives! He does not desire to withhold but to protect, to guide, and to provide! In forbidding us from eating of the Tree of Knowledge of Good and Evil, God sought to protect us. The fear of the Lord is the beginning of knowledge (Prov. 1:7). Taking from the forbidden tree implies that man knows better than God and that we can decide for ourselves what is best for us. We do have a role, but our role in the discovery process is first to be in relationship with God through Jesus Christ. Believing in God and knowing about Him are good, but knowing God and experiencing Him are essential to discovering how fulfill our desires.

I pray that the Lord will minister to you as you read this book and that He will reveal the direction you seek for your life. It is vital to know that our purpose begins with a relationship with Jesus, the lover of our souls. He desires that we take from the Tree of Life, and not from the tree that leads to death. His redeeming power can reveal our direction and our purpose.

Jesus' invitation to His disciples to "follow me" (Matt. 4:19–20; 16:24) remains crucial to discovering our purpose today. He delights in us, and His good pleasure is to guide us to our calling. But do we seek to please the Lord with our lives and with the choices we make? Or do we seek to please only ourselves? How we answer these questions determines whether we are fulfilling our purpose or pursuing things that will leave us less than satisfied and even in distress. It is imperative that we seek to please the Lord, align ourselves with Him, and follow hard after God. In our day and age, we must follow Him without fail, since the forces of the world and the Evil One are growing stronger. It takes strength and courage to surrender to God and to fulfill our purpose.

Tap into your dream, align it with the Lord Jesus, allow Him to adjust it if need be, and then watch Him empower you! Surrender to His still, small voice as you take this journey, and you may be surprised and energized by His touch.

CHAPTER 1

Defining Purpose

For we are His workmanship, created in Christ Jesus for good works, which God prepared beforehand so that we would walk in them.

—Eph. 2:10

Science cannot decide the purpose of life; we need philosophy or religion for that.

—Berger, 2011, 7

My wife once received a package containing a strange item. It was metal, measured about eight inches long, was wavy and curvy, and had a hole at one end. When she showed it to me, I asked what is was. She said she didn't know. My wife was hoping I knew.

We asked a few other people if they knew what the item was, but no one had ever seen anything like it before. We then started taking guesses from our family and friends. We made a list with people's names and their guesses as to what this mystery item was. One person believed it was a shoe horn. Another thought it was a bottle cap opener, even though the hole was too large to fit most bottle caps. We made the guessing fun and sweetened the pot by offering five dollars for the correct answer.

We had an item, and no one knew its purpose. It sat on our kitchen counter for weeks, not being used for anything. One member of my family suggested we give it to Goodwill, since we surely could not use it. But would the Goodwill staff know the purpose of the item? After a while, my wife finally relented and asked her sister, who had sent the item to us. My sister-in-law revealed to us what the object was and expressed surprise that no one had seen such a thing before. Once we all knew and had chuckled about the uniqueness of the item, most of us said, "Of course. That makes perfect sense." Its purpose was to slip over the top of a wine bottle, holding the bottle in place while the cork was removed.

Consider the progressive thinking in our little dilemma. We had an item that none of us had seen before, and we didn't know its purpose. We then asked others to help us identify the item and its purpose. No one else knew either. We made many guesses about the object's purpose. We even thought about giving it away or throwing it out, because we believed it had no purpose. Even though the item had a purpose, when we didn't think it did, we wanted to get rid of it. Eventually, we went to the source—the giver of the item, my sister-in-law. Once we heard from the source, not only did we learn the item's purpose, but its use made perfect sense to us. We pictured the purpose and then used the item accordingly, and sure enough, it worked as it was designed.

We all have been created for a purpose. "Deep within our souls there's a sincere desire for God to use us, a desire imparted to us from God Himself. Woven into our spiritual DNA is a beautiful calling and divine purpose for us to fulfill" (Larson 2013, 120). Knowing our purpose helps bring meaning to our lives.

Unfortunately, when we don't know our purpose, we may feel frustrated, directionless, and as if others want to throw us out or give us away. We feel lost and we often despair when we believe we lack direction. We may feel put aside and useless.

Ultimately, we need to go to the source, God our Creator, to discover what we were designed for. Once we learn our purpose, we may say to ourselves, *Of course. That makes perfect sense.* The Lord has a plan for our lives, and He knows how to help us find fulfillment.

The *American Heritage Dictionary* defines purpose as "the reason for which something exists or happens" or "by design or intentionally" or "an intended or desired result." Other attributes of purpose include aspiration, planning, direction, conviction, motivation, resolve, and intentions. "Human beings have a need to be generative, instrumental, and to achieve great things" (Berger 2011, 625). In 1969, Norman Mailer interviewed astronaut Neil Armstrong, the first man to step on the surface of the moon. Mailer asked him why going to the moon was so important. Armstrong answered, "I think we're going to the moon because it's in the nature of the human being to face challenges. It's by the nature of his deep inner soul … we're required to do these things just as salmon swim upstream" (Heffernan, 2012).

Generativity is directly linked to the intrinsic rewards of working. Intangible benefits such as a sense of accomplishment, the impact on others, appreciation, and gratitude are some of the rewards we experience when we work with integrity. Extrinsic rewards for work such as money and health benefits are not the only benefits of being productive.

Our purpose is found in our passion and our calling. We all have something we care a great deal about. That's our passion. Bugbee suggests three categories of life passions: passions about people (e.g., children, the elderly, the handicapped), passions about roles and functions (e.g., entrepreneur, consultant, designer), and passions for a cause such as human rights, fighting world hunger, or reaching the spiritually lost (Bugbee 1995, 35–36). Our passion can develop into a calling, then into a specific way in which our calling can be expressed. Once we operate within our calling, we fulfill our purpose.

None of us cares about everything equally. One thing usually seems to rise to the top. Our passions come from our inner being, and ultimately God places them there. Bugbee says:

> Sometimes we think of our passion in terms of a *burden* we carry, a *call* we've received, a *dream* we have, or a *vision* we've glimpsed. Whatever you call it, *passion is the God-given desire of the heart to make a difference somewhere"* (original emphasis)(Bugbee 995, 30).

Purpose has a dream behind it and a desired result. We may aspire to become a business owner, a nurse, a missionary, or a police officer. When we wish to be something, we find ourselves motivated to do whatever it takes to get there. We become convinced of our calling, and we then develop a plan. We resolve to see the plan through, convinced what we envision will eventually come to pass.

God created us for a purpose. He has a plan for each of us, and He desires to help us achieve the intended result. He is motivated by love to help us fulfill our purposes, but He waits for us to get with the program. His program begins with us surrendering to Him so He can lead and equip us for His purpose. To live with no purpose will still result in an outcome, but it will most likely be less than what we would desire.

Viktor Frankl (1905–97) was an Austrian psychiatrist who became one of the key figures in existential therapy and a great inspiration for humanistic psychologists. During World War II, members of Frankl's immediate family were deported to Nazi concentration camps because they were Jews. He lost his father, mother, brother, and wife to the Nazi death camps. He and his sister Stella were the only family members who survived. Frankl spent almost three years in concentration camps, from September 1942 to April 1945.

Frankl devoted his career to studying an existential approach to therapy and had apparently concluded that a lack of meaning is the paramount existential stress. To him, existential neurosis was synonymous with a crisis of meaninglessness (Yalom 1980). In other words, Frankl believed the core longing for purpose is the most important human desire.

After enduring the suffering of concentration camps, Frankl validated his hallmark conclusion that even in the most absurd, painful, and dehumanized situation, life has potential meaning and therefore even suffering is meaningful. He said, "What is to give light must endure burning" (Frankl 2006).

Frankl's philosophy is consistent with the life of Jesus, as Peter describes it in his epistle. He wrote:

> Therefore, since Christ has suffered [death] in the flesh, arm yourselves also with the same purpose, because he who has suffered [death] in the flesh has ceased from sin, so as to live the rest of the time in the flesh no longer for the lusts of men, but for the will of God (emphasis mine) (I Peter 4:1-2).

Our flesh and self-centeredness is to die in order for our true purpose to emerge. The more we die to the sinful desires, the more we will experience our true purpose on earth to reflect Christ.

Frankl is thought to have coined the term *Sunday neurosis*. The term refers to a form of anxiety resulting from people's awareness of the emptiness in their lives once the workweek is over. (This is in contrast with the sense of Sabbath, which I will discuss in chapter 4.) Some complain of a void and a vague discontent. This arises from an existential vacuum, or feeling of meaninglessness, a common phenomenon characterized by boredom, apathy, and emptiness. One feels cynical, lacks direction, and questions the point of most of life's activities (Yalom 1980).

Consider Frankl's view as it relates to unemployment. Joblessness, which can feed a sense of having no purpose, has a devastating effect on the individual, his or her family, and society. The emptiness that exists in those who feel as if they aren't contributing to society or to their families can be difficult to overcome. An unemployed client once wrote to me, saying,

> In my current situation I am not working. Not working has really left me feeling as if I do not contribute anything to not only my life, but more so to those around me. I can share that in my personal situation I lack human interaction, and I find that when I am around others (mostly strangers) I feel awkward and unsettled. I am not used to engaging in conversation with others, and the most notable thing of it is I feel inferior. Inferior because I do not work and tend to view myself in a negative way. I have always worked since high school, and I felt good about myself no matter the occupation.

People may contribute to society's ills by choosing not to work when they are able. Research has shown that unemployment is associated with higher rates of problems such as child abuse, alcoholism, and depression (Berger 2011, 625). Proverbs 29:18 says, "Where there is no vision [revelation, purpose], the people are unrestrained." If people maintain stable employment, then individuals, families, and society have a lot to gain. "Individuals seek to satisfy their needs through a combination of intimate relationships, caregiving, and employment" (Berger 2011, 625).

Many people are trying to find out who they are. My book *Created for Significance* discusses how to find or to restore identity. Who we are becomes essential in developing what we do. Some individuals express themselves to find out who they are. I've noticed that many people are anxious, self-centered, defensive, rebellious, and not at peace because they seek who they are in their expressions and behaviors. This concept is backward. As a result, many of these people live with anxiety, make selfish decisions, lack fulfillment, and suffer contentiousness and unrest.

Rest and contentment come when we have discovered who we are, freeing us to manifest our purpose, which is a reflection of this identity. We find true rest when we express in creative forms who we are.

A relationship with our Creator, who has a purpose for each one of us, is essential in discovering our purpose. Peace ultimately is not a place. It is a person! The Prince of Peace, Jesus (Isa. 9:6; Acts 5:30–31), has all intentions of leading us to our purpose. But it starts with Him.

We often struggle with how to find our purpose. We often wait for a sign or for confirmation. Many times we simply expect someone to tell us what to do. We do not take responsibility for getting to know ourselves, or more important, getting to know God, to find our purpose. A woman I worked with once wrote about her journey toward purpose.

> I knew what I wanted to be when I was in middle school. Mainly because my grandmother had rather high hopes

for me since I was her first grandchild. She always told me that she could see me following a judicial career and being a judge. I had decided that I would follow that path to make my grandmother proud of me. However, she passed away five months before I graduated high school. I never went on with my plans to attend law school. Instead I went through a stage where I took a year off from school to search myself and find what I really wanted out of life. I kept putting off college and jobs until I finally decided what I wanted to do with my life.

The loss of her grandmother was a double loss—a person close to her and her purpose. That purpose was attached to her grandmother so that when her grandmother died, so did the woman's purpose, or so it seemed. She got past what someone else had said she should be and so discovered God and His purpose for her. She overcame her loss, and then she found direction. First she found God, and then she found her purpose. This person had decided to become a counselor when we met. While taking classes was a challenge, the purpose she had discovered through her relationship with God and by deepening that relationship gave her great determination.

God desires us to seek Him. A Scripture passage that is often quoted is Jeremiah 29:11–13:

> For I know the plans that I have for you, declares the Lord, plans for welfare and not for calamity to give you a future and a hope. Then you will call upon Me and come and pray to Me, and I will listen to you. And you will seek Me and find Me, when you search for Me with all your heart.

This well-known passage is often used to encourage us when we are struggling. The second part, however, is often overlooked. Do we call upon God? Do we seek Him with all our hearts? Or do we simply plow full steam ahead and then ask God to sanction what we have already chosen to do? That approach is common among those who are not willing to wait on God or to trust Him. However, to discover our purpose, we must seek God!

We can ask God to reveal to us what He desires. We can ask Him to call us to something. We may have a desire that we need to lay before the Lord for Him to confirm, to guide us in, or to allow for change. Matthew 14:22–33 describes the scene when Jesus walked on the water and Peter did the same. The interesting part is that Peter asked to be called! Verse 28 records, "And Peter answered Him and said, 'Lord, if it is You, command me to come to You on the water.' And He said, 'Come!' And Peter got out of the boat, and walked on the water and came toward Jesus." Other Bible translations have Peter saying, "Bid me to come" or "Call me to come."

Jesus complied with Peter's request and called him to come and walk on the water. Though we seem to focus on Peter eventually sinking, we cannot overlook the fact that he did walk on water for a few moments. Peter began to sink when he took his eyes off of Jesus! Peter asked to be called, Jesus beckoned him, and Peter fulfilled the call—at least for a time.

Our purpose is our calling. Do you believe you are called? Have you asked God to call you? Have you asked Him to reveal your purpose? Do you believe you are called to something? Being called is not just for those who want to pursue ministry. We all are called to something. When we are saved through faith in Christ, we are not just saved *from* something (sin, rebellion) but *for* something! God wants to use you. He has a specific assignment that will bring you fulfillment. You simply need to be with Him, to walk with Him, and to ask Him. "Your calling and mine are anchored in God Himself" (Larson 2013, 36). Be prepared for your calling. It may take months, years, or decades before you see your purpose fulfilled.

Several vocations require a person to be on call. Nurses, police officers, doctors, firefighters, pastors, and public utility workers are among those facing this requirement. When we are on call, we know that we could be summoned to an emergency and that we must be ready. We know we will be fulfilling our purpose when our phone rings or when our pager beeps. The truth is, we often may know our purpose but have not been called to fulfill it. We may be prepared, but our beeper hasn't gone off yet. It is God's call to make. "It takes maturity and humility to first awaken to God's desire and then to humbly await His timing" (Larson 2006, 60). We may know our purpose but have to wait until the right time to fulfill it.

Waiting on God for our purpose to be fulfilled is not easy, especially if we know that purpose. Not knowing is difficult, but when we know it and don't see it fulfilled, we can become weary waiting for the manifestation. I was called into ministry when I was seventeen. It was clear to me that God had spoken a purpose for my life. I envisioned a traditional pathway to get there. Man, was I off the mark. My journey involved decades-long frustration and at times a discouraging wait. I wanted the result so much that I usually did not appreciate the countless day-to-day lessons that I learned and that God used to prepare me. There were times when I cried out to God, "What are you doing, Lord? Why is this happening to me? How long do I have to wait? When will this struggle/disappointment end?"

The love of my wife and my children and the love I had for them helped me through the hard times. I thoroughly enjoyed investing in my children and spending time with them as they developed into adulthood. My purpose included enjoying and investing in my family, which is a high calling indeed, perhaps the highest. I realized along the way that being a husband and father was the primary part of my purpose. To this day, the most cherished title that I have is not pastor, doctor, counselor, teacher, coach, or elder. It's dad! God continued to mold me through my family, just as He was using me and my wife to mold our children, even through mistakes, shortcomings, and disappointments. That time helped me to understand the concepts found in my book *Created for Covering*.

Looking back on those many years, I see the divine wisdom and preparation for my calling and what I am doing now. The disappointments, the traumatic events, the vocational frustrations, the joys of family life and adventures together, and the seemingly insignificant experiences have prepared me for today. "If we get so focused on our kingdom-call that we miss the daily-call, we will be susceptible to selfish ambition, self-centeredness, and a self-important view of our role in God's kingdom work" (Larson 2013, 32). God's daily call, as mundane and as unrelated to our overall purpose as it may seem to be, is a preparation for a greater good. The seasons of life teach us, equip us, and mold us for what lies ahead, even when we do not know what that will be.

I experienced unemployment, underemployment, white-collar jobs, blue-collar jobs, no-collar jobs, day shifts, night shifts, grunt work, management positions, retail, labor positions, teaching and coaching in public and private schools, long hours, finishing degrees while working and raising a family, church ministry, secular work, working alone, working with all kinds of people, being a Mr. Mom, working several part-time jobs at once to make ends meet, relationship struggles, death in my family—both natural and tragic—and dealing with family members' addictions, depression, and traumatic events.

I changed my college major twice and started down certain paths, only to hit a dead end each time and be detoured. I became a frustrated man, looking for direction and purpose—and I was a

Christian! As Christians, aren't we supposed to know all the answers to life's questions? Are we not supposed to immediately understand everything we are dealing with? Not! Several times I placed my hope in people who I thought would plow the way on my behalf. Each time I experienced disappointment. I felt overlooked, defeated, and discouraged.

Then I heard God clearly speak to my spirit, saying, "Yes, you have been overlooked, but what are you going to do about it?" I took that to heart. First, I appreciated that God let me know He knew the disappointments and hurt that I experienced. This encouraged me. His affirmation that I felt overlooked and defeated was strangely comforting to me. I knew He understood. But the more significant part of the message was that I had to do something. I knew God was calling me to draw closer to Him and to depend upon Him. That was what I had to do, first and foremost. Actually, all I had to do was to surrender to Him, seek Him, trust Him, and rest in Him. Surrender runs counter to our human nature, which encourages us to take for ourselves.

As I waited on the Lord, He revealed to me what was truly on my heart, my passion. Once He showed me this, I sought Him for ways to express it. God led me to return to school for graduate work, even though I did not know how I was going to afford it. I found that as I followed Him, He made a way where there was none, and with scholarships and grants, I completed graduate work in my passion— ministry, specifically expressed in counseling and teaching.

One day, God cut me to the quick with 2 Timothy 2:24 KJV: "And the Lord's servant must not strive; but be gentle unto all men, apt to teach, patient." I remember thinking, *Aren't we supposed to strive after the things of God?* He was teaching me that we need to strive after Him. Striving after a relationship with Jesus allows the Lord to impart to us His purpose for our lives. I realized that seeking Him would reveal what He had in store for me.

The Greek word for *strive* in 2 Timothy 2:24 is also translated as "quarrel" or to be "contentious." Often, that is what occurs when we strive too hard to prove ourselves—we become contentious, competitive, and insecure in the process. This is as true in the church, in ministries, and among Christians seeking position as it is in the world. Many take on the posture believing no one is going to stop me from doing what I want to do. Right?

When we think we know what we want, or when we are trying hard to prove to others that we are somebody, we fall into the trap of pride, presumption, and contentiousness, which can lead to resentment. That feeling occurs when we don't get what we want when we want it. As a result, we may lose out on what we were striving for. We instead must strive for humility before God, dependence upon Him, and a posture of surrender to allow Him to work in our lives.

The Old Testament prophet Elisha followed hard after his mentor, Elijah. Mentors are helpful in our development, but they are not our all-in-all. Elijah corrected Elisha, making sure he understood that he needed to follow hard after God if he was to experience the double portion of the Spirit that he requested from Elijah (2 Kings 2:1–14). Elisha thought Elijah was the source of his future. Once he saw that Elijah was just a God-anointed man (vv. 12–13) and that the anointing came from the Lord (v. 14), he was able to experience the purpose for which he asked. The double portion of the Spirit was not Elijah's to give. It came from knowing God.

Ruth followed hard after her mother-in-law, Naomi, but she also followed hard after God, as her confession suggests. "Your people shall be my people, and your God, my God" (Ruth 1:16). Ruth's honoring of her mother-in-law and of God became evident to Boaz.

Boaz asked Ruth to be his wife, and she was ultimately blessed for she became a part of the Messianic blood line.

Peter followed hard after Jesus despite denying Him later. When many disciples began to leave Jesus because they didn't understand aspects of His teachings, He turned to the twelve whom he handpicked and asked, "You do not want to go away also, do you?" Peter's response is a great confession for us all today. "Lord, to whom shall we go? You have words of eternal life" (John 6:66–69).

As I surrendered my ambitions, ceased striving, and learned how to rest in Him, believing that He would work on my behalf, I heard Him say to me, "Enough! You will not be overlooked again!" Before I heard the Lord say that, I had to surrender to Him.

After many years, I can honestly say God has kept His promise. He has orchestrated many little things and some big things on my behalf as I have watched Him expand my tent of influence. I have learned to patiently rely on God for the fulfillment of my purpose. I continue to grow in this area. I consider myself a late bloomer, since I found my purpose through many disappointments, twists, and turns in life. I have seen God open many doors, allowing me to teach and to preach and to be a resource for many in ministry and counseling. First, I had to seek Him and to trust Him to unfold His purpose and His best for me.

As a Christian counselor and minister, I have found that I can address most anything that a person or couple may bring to counseling. Because of what God has allowed me to experience, I can speak the language of hurting people in most stages of life and from most backgrounds. Though I never had the honor of serving, when I counsel military personnel, I diligently try to understand and speak their language. I am willing to listen to them and to learn about their lifestyle and their struggles as soldiers, sailors, airmen, or marines. I have a great deal of respect for the men and women of our armed forces, since my father was a World War II combat veteran, as were all my uncles. In addition, I have two sons who serve our country – one as an Airman and one in the Department of Defense in Naval aviation.

Sometimes we may not know what we were made for. Family members or friends may offer their opinions about our purpose. Many people will automatically follow in the footsteps of a parent, a family member, someone they admire, or a close friend to develop their purpose. Sometimes this will lead to one's purpose, but sometimes it will not. We all long to know the reason for our existence. Fowler says, "We require meaning. We need purpose and priorities; we must have some grasp on the big picture" (Fowler 1995, 4). When we do not know our purpose, we often chase after people or things that only seem to provide what we are seeking. When we discover our purpose and pursue it, we feel peace, contentment, and often the presence of God.

The 1981 movie *Chariots of Fire* contrasted Eric Liddell and Harold Abrahams, two gifted runners who won Olympic gold medals in 1924 for Great Britain. Liddell was from a Scottish family that had undertaken a Christian mission to China. Abrahams was from a well-to-do Jewish family in England and attended Cambridge University. Both were world-class sprinters. In the movie, Liddell's sister, Jenny, expressed concern about the distraction that running would be in her brother's life. She wanted him to be solely devoted to his missionary work. He recognized her concerns and invited her to go for a walk in the beautiful hills of Scotland for a heart-to-heart talk.

Liddell's response to his sister's fears revealed his awareness of how God could use his gifts. He told her, "I believe God made me for a purpose—for China. But He also made me fast! And when I run,

I feel His pleasure." What a powerful statement! His Olympic gold medal enhanced his effectiveness in China, and Scotland respected the Liddell family. When we are in God's purpose, using the talents He has given us, we will bring glory to Him and know His pleasure. That is true peace and contentment.

Abrahams, on the other hand, was depicted in *Chariots of Fire* as a frustrated man with a chip on his shoulder. He competed for a different reason—to prove to the world that he was not inferior to others. His intent was more related to self-justification and self-glory. In one scene in the movie, Abrahams discusses his drive for success with Aubrey Montague, a teammate who did not win a medal in a steeplechase event and yet remained amiable and pleasant. Abrahams said:

> You, Aubrey are my most complete man. You're kind. You're compassionate. A content man. Contentment! That is your secret! I'm twenty-four (years old) and I've never known it! I'm forever in pursuit, and I don't even know what it is I'm chasing. (parenthesis mine)

Quite a sad revelation for a world-class athlete or for anyone else. "I'm forever in pursuit, and I don't even know what it is I'm chasing" Abrahams said. His confession belongs to anyone who has not found his or her purpose. Perhaps that is your confession. However, God can change that.

We may eventually find a greater purpose than athletics, music, the military, or business. When we discover we are good at something and enjoy success in that area, we may have found part of our purpose. Liddell is a good example. His athletic gifts and success enhanced his effectiveness for the gospel. Athletics, music, business ownership, ministry, or any other call in life may be a part of our purpose. John McCain and Colin Powell, who served in the military in Vietnam, continued their public service in Congress and on a president's cabinet, respectively.

There is often a larger part to play beyond our current pursuits. I will discuss this in subsequent chapters. Tim Tebow is an example. He was a college football player won two national championships (2007 and 2009), earned the Heisman Trophy award (2007), was drafted into the National Football League, and had some success in the NFL. His fame has placed him in the international spotlight, allowing him to present Jesus Christ to parts of the world that others are not able to enter. Other world-class Christian athletes, such as Steve Largent (NFL), Jim Ryun (Olympic runner and medalist), and J. C. Watts (college football star), have served our nation in Congress after their athletic careers and have become positive examples for the kingdom of God.

We can also feel God's pleasure, since our purpose in life is given to us by God Himself. True rest and contentment are found when we give expression to who we are. If we are living according to someone else's expectations and purpose for our lives, we may never find peace and contentment. If we express someone else's vision, we will not feel the same contentment and sense of purpose that we would feel if it had been our own. Someone else's purpose is not our purpose. Unfortunately, many people never discover their purpose, and they live frustrating lives.

Some people may know early in their lives what they are meant to be. Three of my five children fall into that category. One of my sons, from as early as five years old, knew he wanted to fly planes. He would sketch or trace lots of planes and space shuttles as a youngster. My wife and I recognized this early and encouraged him in his desire. At seventeen, he earned his private pilot's license. Today he is a pilot for a major airline.

When my oldest daughter was a youngster, she wanted to be a nurse like her mother, but she was discouraged from pursuing nursing because of drawbacks such as stressful shifts, poor hospital policies, and lack of respect among many doctors. Her nurturing nature redirected her to consider animal science. However, after two years in college as an animal science major, she knew her purpose was to be a nurse, and she changed her major. Once she completed nursing school she began working as a hospital nurse.

My youngest daughter has loved children from the time she was a child. She would line up her stuffed animals and her dolls in rows in her bedroom and pretend to be their teacher. From her early days, she wanted to teach young children. She loved serving in our church nursery and would babysit many children. She was sometimes considered one of the family by the parents of the children she cared for. She received a teaching fellowship to college as others recognized her passion and her purpose. Today she is an elementary school teacher. She is particularly passionate about students with special needs and loves what she does.

Our other two sons discovered their direction as they went. Both serve our nation's military. Both changed their college majors and continue to see their purpose unfold despite bumps in the road. These young men have more in common with most people as it relates to finding a purpose. We discover it as we go through life's disappointments, twists, and turns. That was true for me as well.

Many times we discover our purpose because of the influence of a loved one. We may choose to be an accountant because a parent was one. Perhaps a favorite uncle or aunt was a doctor or a teacher, and so we decided that our purpose was to be like them. We may be influenced by a traumatic event. I know a woman who became a neurosurgeon because as a teenager, she helped care for a favored grandmother who died of a brain condition. Many of my high school classmates had such good experiences with their teachers or coaches that they pursued education and became teachers and coaches.

So what is your purpose? Do you feel God's pleasure in what you do? Is the pursuit of purpose your way of defining who you are? Do you know who you are, and have you found ways to express it, thereby living your purpose? These are important questions that I pray can be answered through your journey. When you do not know who you are, you do not know what to do. When you know who you are, you know what to do. When you forget who you are, you forget what to do. When you remember who you are, you know what to do. So who do you think you are? You need to ask this question before you answer the question, "What should I do?"

Most people will answer the identity question by explaining what they have, what they do, who they know, or what has been done to them. And while these things may explain someone, they do not define the person. Do not let outside forces or other people define who you are. You need to learn who you are before you can know what to do, because your activity proceeds from your identity. It is never too late to find and to live your purpose. As long as you have breath, you can discover who you are, what you should do, and where you are going. It all begins with God.

God's purpose for our lives was established in the beginning. Our hearts will determine who we are and where we are going. Proverbs 16:9 (KJV) says, "A man's heart deviseth his way, but the Lord directeth his steps." It is essential, therefore, to surrender our hearts to the Lord in order to follow Him toward our purpose. However, sin separates us from Him.

When people are separated from God, restlessness and loneliness draw them to seek fulfillment of God-given longings in destructive ways. Idleman says, "He hates everything that becomes an obstacle between you and Him, everything that blocks your view of Him or threatens to keep you from hearing His voice. He wants you, and not just some of you" (Idleman 2013, 51). Proverbs 4:23 (NIV) says, "Above all else, guard your heart, for everything you do flows from it." The Bible also says, "As water reflects the face, so one's life reflects the heart" (Prov. 27:19 NIV).

The Lord has established ways to measure our hearts: His Word and His laws. He also has provided the way to change our hearts to line up with His: through grace and the finished work of Jesus Christ. "The issue is not what we are, but who He is" (Joyner 1993, 45).

The next chapter will focus on God and His foundational purpose for our lives.

CHAPTER 2

God's Purpose for Us

He has told you, O man, what is good; and what does the Lord require of you but to do justice, to love kindness, and to walk humbly with your God.

—Mic. 6:8

I, the Lord, search the heart, I test the mind, even to give to each man according to his ways, according to the results of his deeds.

—Jer. 17:10

This book of the Law shall not depart from your mouth, but you shall meditate on it day and night, so that you may be careful to do according to all that is written in it; for then you will make your way prosperous, and then you will have success.

—Josh. 1:8

I n 2002, Rick Warren, pastor of Saddleback Church in Lake Forest, California, wrote a national best-seller called *The Purpose Driven Life*. His book struck a nerve. When we consider that it was a number- one best-seller for almost two years, in 2004 and 2005, we realize that many people are indeed seeking purpose in their lives.

Most people have felt the need to discover their purpose, and Pastor Warren tapped into that desire through his forty-day devotional framework. The five themes in the book are as follows.

- You were planned for God's pleasure.
- You were formed for God's family.
- You were created to become like Christ.
- You were shaped for serving God.
- You were made for a mission. (Warren, 2002)

I want to underscore that we all desire to know our purpose. That is a human core longing. Just like every other core longing that I write about in this series, it begins with a relationship with God through Jesus Christ. We were made to *belong* to God; to *love* and to be loved; to be *safe* and secure in relationships and in God; to *understand* and to be understood; to be like God, to reflect Him, and by doing so, to have *significance*, to make an impact, and to be fruitful for the greater good, showing forth our *purpose*.

God's attributes provide us with a way to understand His purpose. That purpose is directly related to who He is. The same is true of us. Our purpose is directly related to who we are. Thus, to know and to understand our purpose, we need to know and to understand who we are. To know who we are, we need to recognize that our identity and significance are in God. (For a complete discussion of our identity, see the first book in this series, *Created for Significance*.)

First and foremost, we are created in God's image and we belong to Him. If we do not know God, we may struggle with our purpose, since our purpose is to reflect God. G. K. Beale, a leading professor of biblical theology at Wheaton College Graduate School, says, "All humans have been created to be reflecting beings, and they will reflect whatever they are ultimately committed to, whether the true God or some other object in the created world" (Beale 2008, 22).

Just as the moon has no light of its own but reflects the sun's light, we do not have light or life of our own doing. We are to reflect God. Jesus said in Matthew 5:16, "Let your light shine before men in such a way that they may see your good works, and glorify your Father who is in heaven." Our purpose is directly linked to our identity with God, for we are to glorify Him with our lives. Calvin said, "There is no deep knowing of God without a deep knowing of self and no deep knowing of self without a deep knowing of God" (Calvin 1995, 15). So let's begin by discussing some of God's attributes further.

The Bible opens by saying, "In the beginning, God created the heavens and the earth" (Gen. 1:1). God's character leads to His purpose. One of His attributes is that of creator, so He created. He had a purpose and a design. The first few chapters of the book of Genesis establish God's purpose for human beings and give us a glimpse of that plan. The Lord was intentional in His creation. The earth and the universe did not come into existence by accident or by a random "bang."

Science, especially evolutionary science, seems to argue that the universe somehow simply occurred. As long as God is kept out of the equation, the universe has no design or purpose. If the universe has no design or purpose, then neither does the emergence of humankind. We are therefore left to believe that human beings automatically sprang into existence with no design or purpose. We just happened!

Evolutionary science has done a disservice to humankind by devaluing human life. After all, what greater value can we find in ourselves than knowing that we are created for a purpose, especially a purpose that is linked to our Creator's design? If human beings just evolved, how can we possibly discover and explain our purpose?

Our purpose is directly related to God's purpose for us. Therefore, to achieve our purpose in life, it is essential to know that we were created intentionally and to submit to God's purpose for us.

The Bible makes it clear that God created man and woman with a purpose. He planned to accomplish much through the righteous seed of humanity. The purpose of human beings is to bring glory to God through service, obedience, and worship and to have an impact upon creation in all that we do. After He created the earth, its foliage, beasts and birds, God made human beings. Genesis 1:26–28 says:

> Then God said, "Let Us make man in Our image, according to our likeness; and let them rule over the fish of the sea and over the birds of the sky and over the cattle and over all the earth, and over every creeping thing that creeps on the earth." God created man in His own image, in the image of God He created him; male and female He created them. God blessed them; and God said to them, "be fruitful and multiply, and fill the earth, and subdue it; and rule over the fish of the sea and over the birds of the sky and over every living thing that moves on the earth."

God is Creator. By nature, God as Creator brings forth life. Though scientists attempt to discover the origins of the universe exclusively through science, ultimately a grand designer had to begin the process of what we know to be life, even in its simplest forms. Because it is in God's nature to create, He purposed to create, and He created—He brought forth life. His purpose is a manifestation of who He is. Genesis 2:7 says, "Then the Lord God formed man of dust from the ground, and breathed into his nostrils the breath of life; and man became a living being."

We are also created to create. Many people throughout history have created to better the human race. Art, music, and inventions to make our lives easier are just a few of the things people have created. All too often, we ignore or dismiss as unimportant the creative dimension of our lives in Christ. Imagine how empty our lives would be within the realm of Christendom without artists, musicians, scientists, poets, and the like. However, again all too often, creativity is confined to the arts and the humanities to the exclusion of administration, technology, economics, business, science, social science, education, and the list could go on. God is the creative genius behind it all! To create is part of our purpose. We cannot make something out of nothing—creation in its truest sense—but we can bring to life something that did not exist before.

Because He gave us the ability to create, God designed marriage to be between a man and a woman. Sexual relations only between a man and a woman can bring forth life. When a man and a woman have intercourse, a new life can begin. We have no right to alter God's design and to redefine marriage as something other than the relationship between a man and a woman. Something opposed to God's design will not bring forth life. The Creator has graciously allowed humans to participate in life-giving through the love between a man and a woman. That is a part of our purpose. Same-sex relationships will not fulfill the purpose that we have in God, because they cannot bring forth life and will lead to frustration, anguish, unfulfillment, and even death.

Besides the work of creating life, God is calling us to a new life—a life in Him. Living life in God's kingdom brings much more fulfillment than living life in the world. We do not get new life through religion. We obtain it through relationship. "Jesus did the same thing throughout His ministry. He was not calling people to a new religion or a new ethical system; He was, as Bonhoeffer says, calling people to life" (Boyd 2004, 95).

The Lord is also a relational God. The doctrine of the Trinity underscores such a characteristic of God. One of the Hebrew words used for God in the Old Testament is *Elohim*, and it is a plural word. When the Lord decided to create human beings, He said, "Let Us make man in Our image, according to Our likeness" (Gen. 1:26). God, as represented in the Father, Son, and Holy Spirit, has been in relationship with Himself for eternity. Thus His creation reflects a relational dimension.

The animal kingdom relates within its own species. Genesis 1:21–25 makes it clear that God created sea creatures, birds, and land animals all after their own kind. Human beings were created to relate to each other. God made male and female of every kind for heterosexual relationships and to reproduce. Without relationship, no animal or human would survive or reproduce. We may believe that being isolated is good, but God determined that it is not good for man to be alone (Gen. 2:18).

God is also almighty. He makes an impact. All God had to do was say, "Let there be light," and there was light (Gen 1:5). That is quite an impact. He spoke it and it was. If there was a big bang, it was because God spoke, and bang, it came to be! All of creation was designed and established by an almighty, loving God. Everything in nature has an order to it. In fact, there is too much of an order for anyone to seriously consider a random beginning for the universe, our world, and human life. Man was designed with a purpose in mind—to be like God. He formed man from the dust of the ground, breathed into his nostrils, and made him a living being (Gen. 2:7). The powerful truth that we are made in God's image can establish self-esteem and humility at the same time.

Like God, we were created to make an impact. God said that man would rule over the other creatures of the earth and told him to be fruitful and multiply (Gen. 1:26–28). That refers directly to the call to procreate and to fill the earth with people who also love God and who can be stewards and developers of His creation.

The call to be fruitful also refers to the responsibility to be productive and to serve God and one another for the greater good. Our work exists to support humanity as an expression of obedience and to fulfill God's intent for His creation (Sherman and Hendricks 1987). This was God's design and humanity's purpose. Doing so would require human beings to make a growing impact upon creation and on one another. Unfortunately, God's plan was derailed by Satan when he convinced Adam and Eve to divert from the Lord's intentions. This will be discussed further in chapter 7.

Finally, God said that He is a holy God. He also said we are to be holy as He is holy (Lev. 11:44; 19:2; 20:7). Several times in the New Testament the writers reiterate this truth. For example, Paul writes that we are temples of the Holy Spirit, "for the temple of God is holy, and that is what you are" (1 Cor. 3:16–17). Peter writes, "But like the Holy One who called you, be holy yourselves also in your behavior; because it is written, 'You shall be holy, for I am holy'" (1 Peter 1:15–16).

To be holy does not mean to be perfect. To be holy does not mean that we earn eternal life through our behavior. To be holy is not only about outward appearances. The love of God transforms us to live lives of holy purpose. Boyd says:

> The New Testament is not about ethical behavior; it's about a radical new way of living. It is about life lived in surrendered union to God through faith in Jesus Christ. It is about experiencing the transforming power of God's love flowing into and through a person. It demands a form of holiness that is far more exacting than any ethical or religious system. It demands the holiness of the heart (Boyd 2004, 96).

The Hebrew word *qadash* and the Greek word *hosios*, used often in the Scriptures, have similar meanings. They mean to be "set apart" or to "consecrate" or to "purify." The idea is that the one who is holy is set apart as different from anything else. We know we are different when we experience the love of the Father. "His purpose was not to get us to *act* differently; His goal was to help us to *be* different" (Italics not mine)(Boyd 2004, 94).

God is different from any other god, because He is the Creator and almighty with no beginning and no end. Psalm 90:2 says that God is from everlasting to everlasting. All the gods in other religions have beginning stories. The God of the Bible does not. As such, He is set apart, or holy, because He is different. He is different in countless other ways.

Christians are to be different as well. God is not commanding something that we cannot attain. His command is not about being perfect. It is about being like Him—different from the culture in which we live. Jesus makes it possible to follow after God. Being holy involves much more than the clothes we wear and the rituals we observe. It is about being like Jesus. It is not about trying to be different through our wardrobe and our tattoos. It is about being different because Jesus is making us different.

God has called us to be holy—to be different from the world, to be different in our thinking compared with those who think according to the world, and to be different in our behavior as a positive contrast to those in the world. The problem has increasingly become that those who say they follow Jesus are not very different from those of the world. We Christians do not stand out as much from the world in a positive way as we used to and as we should. Part of our purpose is to be different. But there is a cost to standing out, and many of us are not willing to pay the price. Our purpose becomes muddied when we do not stand out to reflect Jesus.

So, we have several primary purposes for our lives. These purposes are based upon being in God's image and knowing Him. We have a purpose to create and to bring forth life. We have a purpose to be in positive relationships one with another and with God. We have a purpose to be fruitful, to make a positive impact, and to be effective for the greater good of others.

These purposes are at the core of every human being. When we sense that they are being fulfilled, we experience peace and contentment. These purposes are manifested in many different ways in our lives. When we sense we have not discovered or fulfilled our purpose, we are in turmoil and will often seek to fill the longing with whatever we can find, even if it has hurtful consequences. We need to know what we are to do with our lives, because we all have a tendency to "strive to arrive."

God's Blueprint

When Adam and Eve sinned, they became separated from God, and this caused them to be at odds with Him and with each other. Their actions have affected every human relationship since then. As soon as they ate from the forbidden tree, they knew something was wrong. They knew they had disobeyed God's command to them. How did they know that? As part of their purpose, they were told by God to avoid the Tree of Knowledge of Good and Evil.

The Lord told them to be fruitful and multiply, to take dominion over His creation, and to stay away from the tree (Gen. 1:28; 2:16–17). When Adam and Eve disobeyed, they felt shame and wanted to hide themselves (Gen. 3:7). They also blamed someone else for the breach instead of taking responsibility. Ever since, we have attempted to hide from God in our sin and to justify that sin by blaming someone else. Or, by suggesting that what we did or didn't do was not as bad as how someone else behaved. Such behavior ruins our purpose in life because we spend so much time hiding who we are and blaming others.

God's purpose for us has always included His commands. He provides a blueprint through them. We are called to follow the Lord, and following Him includes walking in His ways. If we break God's commands, we become separated from Him, and our purpose becomes derailed and less than what He had intended.

However, the Lord had a plan of restoration. He prophesied to Adam and Eve that humankind would eventually see a Savior be born into the world to restore a relationship with Him and to reestablish what God had in mind (Gen. 3:14–15). As humanity waited for the promised Messiah to come, God passed on laws for men and women to follow. These laws, or commandments, would help do at least two things: (1) reestablish the Lord's purpose for all people, and (2) reveal to us that we have wandered far from our initial purpose and that we need help, namely a loving Savior, to get to where we need to be.

Most of us have a working knowledge of the Ten Commandments. We may even quote them from time to time in certain situations. However, did you know that they can be seen as God's blueprint for purpose in our lives? The Ten Commandments were provided by God to Moses to reestablish the purpose of human beings in relation to God and to each other.

The Ten Commandments are often understood to be cold, harsh words from an all-powerful and vengeful God. In reality, they are ten declarations of our Creator's love for us. The Ten Commandments are guiding steps that can keep us from being bruised and broken by the deadly snares of a fallen world. They are restraints from a loving

Father on His beloved children. If we understood God's motivation for giving us the commandments, we would see that these restraints bring life and purpose to our lives. If we obey God's commandments, we will be led by His guiding hand and will walk through life with confidence.

God gave the Ten Commandments to Moses at a time of great crisis and rebellion. The nation of Israel was finding its identity on the way to the Promised Land. The people rebelled against their spiritual leader and against their God, affecting their thinking and their direction. Soon after they were freed from slavery, they grumbled and became discontented over the state of their lives. The Hebrews preferred being in slavery to living in freedom through God's direction.

We are at a similar time in history. The church is being compromised, standards are being changed, evil is called good, and good is called evil. The Ten Commandments themselves face criticism. People are trying to remove them from our courtrooms and public squares. Is it any wonder that more and more of us are struggling with meaning in life? There is a direct correlation. Once we remove God's directives and restraints, we invite rebellion, self-centeredness, chaos, and unrestrained evil—which affects everyone!

The commandments are eternal, so they are just as relevant to our lives today as they were in the days of Moses. The commandments lay the foundation of our longing for purpose and can help answer the question, "What am I to do with my life?" From this foundation, there are countless ways for us to manifest the fulfillment of these God-given statutes. I will say more about this in the next few chapters.

Our purpose in life first hinges upon how we view God and who we worship. The question is, who are we ultimately pleasing? Next, our purpose is seen through our dealings with others. The first three commandments focus on our relationship with God. Six commandments convey our purpose in relation to how we are to treat one another. One commandment lays out an attitude that includes a promise and a reward, enhancing or hindering our purpose.

It is interesting to note that the vast majority of psychological theories do not necessarily help us understand our purpose in light of the Ten Commandments. The major theoreticians—Freud, Jung, Erickson, Piaget, Frankl, Rogers, Maslow, and Adler—came from a godless European mindset that emphasized individual self-actualization to varying degrees. "The liberty of self-actualization, not life, has become the most important right an individual can have" (Robertson 2004, 133). In other words, the measure of mental health was achieving self-actualization and individual autonomy. Most other cultures in the world found this approach foreign to them.

Psychiatrist Murray Bowen, influenced by his wartime experience as a medical officer in the army from 1941 to 1945, introduced another approach that made sense to many. The fundamental premise of his theory that differentiates it from traditional psychotherapeutic theory is this: the family is an emotional unit, and any change in the emotional functioning of one member of that unit is predictably and automatically compensated for by changes in the emotional functioning of other members. In other words, the family, and the relationships within the family (or lack thereof), affect the way we relate to others, to ourselves, and ultimately to God. Jay Haley, Salvador Minuchin, and Virginia Satir followed Bowen's lead in their approach to mental health. According to this theory, mental health is not measured by our ability to self-actualize but by how we get along with others.

We discover our identity and significance through relationship with God! Our purpose is placed against a backdrop of relationships.

The Ten Commandments are all about relationships—how we are to conduct ourselves with God and with others. Most other cultures have a better handle on this than the European mindset.

So the Ten Commandments provide a foundational purpose in our lives from which other specific purposes will arise. A psalm of David describes the law of God and how it affects our lives.

> The law of the Lord is perfect, restoring the soul; the testimony of the Lord is sure, making wise the simple. The precepts of the Lord are right, rejoicing the heart; the commandment of the Lord is pure, enlightening the eyes. The fear of the Lord is clean, enduring forever; the judgments of the Lord are true; they are righteous altogether. They are more desirable than gold, yes, than much fine gold; sweeter also than honey and the honey drippings of the honeycomb. Moreover, by them Thy servant is warned; in keeping them there is great reward. Who can discern his errors? Acquit me of hidden faults. Also, keep back Thy servant from presumptuous sins; let them not rule over me; then I shall be blameless, and I shall be acquitted of great transgression. Let the words of my mouth and the meditation of my heart be acceptable in Thy sight, O Lord my rock and my Redeemer. (Ps. 19:7–14)

The psalmist makes it clear that if we abide by the commandments of the Lord we will experience:

- restoration of our souls
- wisdom
- joy in our hearts
- enlightenment
- understanding
- rewards greater than gold

All of us can benefit from these things! They contribute to our purpose. We will clearly see what is right and what is wrong and thus make a more positive impact. Also, consider Psalm 1:2–3:

> But his delight is in the law of the Lord, and in His law he meditates day and night. He will be like a tree firmly planted by streams of water, which yields its fruit in its season, and its leaf does not wither; *and in whatever he does, he prospers* (emphasis mine).

If we are firmly planted by the living water Himself, we will bring forth good fruit. "When you and I walk closely with the Lord, our desires become pure, our goals clearer" (Larson 2013, 45). I am amazed at how often I hear non-Christians say that anyone who truly follows Christ is living a constrained, unrewarding, and boring life. According to these psalms and other Scripture passages, following Jesus results in abundant life.

Abiding in God produces the desire to follow Him and to obey His commandments. Jesus said, "If you love Me, you will keep My commandments" (John 14:15). If we love God, we want to please Him rather than ourselves. Without true love for God, we will have difficulty discovering our purpose, let alone fulfilling it. The laws and the ways of God become a part of our lives when we accept Christ as Lord and Savior. When we surrender to Jesus, the Holy Spirit empowers us to discern the ways of the Lord and to live them.

Psalm 19 says that the law of the Lord is perfect. Therefore it is unwise and often deadly to circumvent His statutes to meet our own criteria. Anything short of following the heart of God will lead us into darkness, disappointment, doubt, despair, and ultimately death. Jesus has made it possible to follow God's ways, because if we are Christians, Jesus lives in us. He said,

> Do not think that I came to abolish the Law or the
> Prophets; I did not come to abolish, but to fulfill. For
> truly I say to you, unless heaven and earth pass away,
> not the smallest letter or stroke shall pass away from
> the Law, until all is accomplished. Whoever annuls one
> of the least of these commandments, and so teaches
> others, shall be called least in the kingdom of heaven; but
> whoever keeps and teaches them, he shall be called great
> in the kingdom of heaven. For I say to you, that unless
> your righteousness surpasses that of the scribes and
> Pharisees, you shall not enter the kingdom of heaven.
> (Matt. 5:17–20)

The law of the Lord is not only an Old Testament concept. It is a New Testament and new covenant way of life as well. The major difference is that Jesus fulfilled the law by His sinless life. Then He laid down His life as a ransom for all in propitiation for all sins (Rom. 3:25; 1 John 2:2). Because of our sinful nature, no one has ever kept the law completely. Since all have sinned and fallen short of the glory of God (Rom. 3:23), the only way to salvation is faith in Jesus. Living the law won't suffice.

In his writings to the Romans, the apostle Paul builds an ironclad case for the efficacy of grace as opposed to the law. He makes it clear that salvation is impossible through the works of the law or by human effort. Paul writes, "Because by the works of the Law no flesh will be justified in His sight; for through the Law comes the knowledge of sin" (Rom. 3:20). Jesus is the only way to eternal life, and all of us must accept what He did on our behalf.

However, while salvation is secured in Jesus, He made it clear that He did not abolish the law. The law was not to be discarded. The problem was not the law but human beings' inability to adhere to it under their own power. Paul writes, "So then, the Law is holy, and the commandment is holy and righteous and good. Therefore did that which is good become a cause of death for me? May it never be! Rather it was sin" (Rom. 7:12–13).

The law revealed sin, which left us unable to live the law completely. Complete adherence to the law was not possible for us because of our inherited sinful nature. That is why we needed a redeemer—someone who would restore our relationship with God and empower us in righteous living. When we accept Christ and understand righteous living, we discover our purpose in life. Faith in Christ is more than just belief—it is transformational! Christianity is ultimately a relationship lifestyle.

Jesus was the only one ever to completely fulfill the requirements of the law. Now, because of the finished work of Christ, the Holy Spirit can provide us with the power to live the lives that God has purposed for us. Through Jesus, not only do we have salvation and new life, but we have the Holy Spirit, who empowers us to fulfill the law as long as we depend on Him to live our lives. While the gospel frees us from obligation to the law for our salvation, our salvation in Christ liberates and empowers us to live like Him to find purpose and fulfillment. While the law reveals much of our purpose, that purpose can be fulfilled only through faith and surrender to Christ.

On our own, we cannot fulfill the requirements of God's commandments. That is what Jesus was referring to when He mentioned the scribes and the Pharisees in Matthew 5:17–20. They had the audacity to believe that they were above others by virtue of living according to God's law and that the common folk had to aspire to be like them. We must give up such self-righteousness, which exists in all those who think they are religious, to live in the kingdom of God. If we truly love God, we will want to follow Him and to live according to His ways.

Being religious won't save us. Buddhists are religious. Muslims are religious. Hindus are religious. Even many Christians are religious. Religion does not bring eternal life—relationship with Jesus does! Religion is man's attempt to get to God. True Christianity is God coming to man. God has always pursued us, like a lover pursues the one he loves. God pursues us for relationship through Jesus. God pursues us to meet our core longings, including the revelation of purpose. Humanity's relationship with God was broken by sin. God desired to restore the relationship and took the initiative to do it.

Men and women walking in sin do not desire relationship with God. Paul quotes Psalms 14 and 53 when he writes, "There is none righteous, not even one; there is none who understands, there is none who seek for God" (Rom. 3:10–11). Relationship with Jesus is the only way to the Father. Jesus initiated relationship with humanity to restore us to the Father. Through faith in Christ we are indeed restored to God. Jesus did not abolish the law. He fulfilled it, and through new life in Him, Jesus gave us the power to fulfill the law as well.

Our salvation is not based upon good works. We do not earn our salvation by living the law. We gain eternal life through Jesus and Him alone. "I am the Way, and the Truth, and the Life; no one comes unto the Father but through Me" (John 14:6). No one is capable of fulfilling the requirements of the law without help. Paul writes, "Because by the works of the Law no flesh will be justified in His sight … for all have sinned and fall short of the glory of God" (Rom. 3:20, 23). Our salvation is a gift of grace through the finished work of Jesus. Once we accept Christ, our salvation results in a desire to live the law. In our salvation in Jesus, transformation takes place. Transformation brings the Holy Spirit into our lives as the power we need for kingdom living. This is a Spirit-led life, not a human-led life. That is true conversion—to desire God and to please Him.

In dealing with the question of salvation, Jesus said, "This is the work of God, that you believe in Him whom he has sent" (John 6:29). Our first and only "work" is to believe in Jesus and to accept Him as our Savior. This is the only way that leads to eternal life. Later Jesus said, "Truly, truly I say to you, he who believes in Me, the works that I do, he will do also; and greater works than these he will do" (John 14:12). Jesus was referring to supernatural works and to the everyday approach we take to live life as we follow Him. Living the law is not possible outside of faith in Jesus and surrender to His Holy Spirit. We are able to live the law through relationship with Christ. He then provides purpose and direction in our lives.

The apostle James made it clear that faith and works are linked. James writes:

> Even so faith, if it has no works, is dead, being by itself ... But are you willing to recognize, you foolish fellow, that faith without works is useless? Was not Abraham our father justified by works when he offered up Isaac his son on the altar? You see that faith was working with his works, and as a result of the works, faith was perfected ... For just as the body without the spirit is dead, so also faith without works is dead" (James 2:17, 20–22, 26).

True devotion to Jesus produces good works—the ability to live out our purpose as God designed it. Living the law becomes possible through Christ. Living a Christ-empowered life makes it seem as if there is no law, because we sense that our lives flow with His life. If Jesus lives in us, we live as He did. We evidence living the law through the fruits of the Spirit: "love, joy, peace, patience, kindness, goodness, faithfulness, gentleness, self-control; against such things there is no law" (Gal. 5:22–23).

Living the law will lead us to our ultimate purpose in life—to reflect Christ and to treat others well. "Remember that God's law is designed for our benefit" (Rosenbaum 1994, 26). Jesus said that a true believer lives the law by following two commandments, which are the essence of all the law. A lawyer once asked Jesus what he needed to do to inherit eternal life, and Jesus returned his question with another question. The exchange is found in Luke 10:25-28:

> And He said to him, "What is written in the Law? How does it read to you?" And he answered, "You shall love the Lord your God with all your heart, and with all your soul, and with all your strength, and with all your mind; and your neighbor as yourself." And He said to him, "You have answered correctly; do this and you will live."

This is the essence of our purpose in life. If we follow these commandments, we will live!

Let's review the Ten Commandments as found in Exodus 20:1–17:

1. You shall have no other gods before me. You shall not make for yourself a graven image, or any likeness of anything that is in heaven above, or that is in the earth beneath, or that is in the water under the earth. You shall not bow down to them or serve them: for I the Lord your God am a jealous God. (He is the Creator, the life-giver, omniscient and omnipresent.)
2. You shall not take the name of the Lord thy God in vain. (There is power, uniqueness, and comfort in God's name.)
3. Remember the Sabbath day, to keep it holy. (It is the day when God rested and when believers rest.)
4. Honor your father and your mother, that your days may be prolonged in the land which the Lord your God gives you. (Ephesians 6:2–3 says, "Honor your father and mother, that

it may be well with you, and that you may live long on the earth." This is the first commandment with a promise.)

5. You shall not murder. (Give and preserve life; do not hate or destroy; Matt. 5:21–22.)

6. You shall not commit adultery. (Remain faithful; be like God, a lover of our souls; Matt. 5:27–28.)

7. You shall not steal. (God has everything; He is the source of all things; God's desire is to give.)

8. You shall not bear false witness against your neighbor. (Tell the truth; avoid false accusations; build up rather than tear down; take responsibility.)

9. You shall not covet your neighbor's house. (Be content and thankful; do not envy or have a sense of entitlement.)

10. You shall not covet your neighbor's wife, or his male servant, or his female servant, or his ox, or his donkey, or anything that belongs to your neighbor. (Do not be driven by lust; avoid a "keeping up with the Joneses" mentality; remain thankful and content; do not strive for power and position over others.)

Orthodox churches and most Protestant churches split the first commandment into two and combine the last two into one. The way that I have spelled out the commandments here is how the Roman Catholic Church and the Lutheran Church understand them. Either way, there are ten.

The knowledge of what is good and what is evil underscores the purpose of our lives. We all have life values by which we conduct our lives. Identity and values develop our purpose. Unfortunately, not all values are based in righteousness. Many are based upon self-centered fulfillments. Some are based upon outright evil, such as when street gangs defend their turf. Defending their turf is a value, and gang members are vigilant about it. To defend their turf, they sometimes resort to assault and murder.

Our purpose is related to what we value, what we worship, and what we desire. The old cliché "Garbage in, garbage out" is so true. Perhaps we need to establish a new cliché, something like this: "Jesus in, Jesus out."

"Where there is no vision, the people are unrestrained, but happy [blessed] is he who keeps the law" (parenthesis mine) (Prov. 29:18).

Chapter 3

Purpose: Relationship with God— Commandments One and Two

God delivered me from the god I think is God.
—Meister Eckhart

There is no one like You among the gods, O Lord, nor are there any works like Yours.
—Ps. 86:8

Call to me and I will tell you great and unsearchable things you do not know.
—Jer. 33:3

In my work as a counselor, I have often heard it said by Christian and non-Christian colleagues and in continuing education classes that we need to maintain a "value-free" approach to counseling. The idea is to be sure that a counselor does not offend a client with values the client doesn't share. The client is to feel safe and judgment-free during counseling.

While I agree that it is essential to provide safety and trust between client and counselor, I believe it is impossible to approach anything in life with a value-free mindset. A client surely has values from which he or she has made decisions. A counselor also has values upon which a clinical approach is based. If there is a conflict between counselor and client, perhaps a referral should be made. If the client has come to counseling because of adverse consequences from life's decisions and circumstances, perhaps a new value system is indeed necessary. No one operates in a vacuum, free from value-based decisions. Some values must be changed to redirect a person's life. That is not judging someone. That is helping someone. (I discuss judging in *Created for Understanding*.)

The same is true about belief in God. Many say they do not believe in God and call themselves atheists, agnostics, or pagans. Atheists and agnostics believe that no deity exists to oversee the universe and the lives of human beings. Pagans may believe in a deity, but it is not the one true God, Creator, and Lord of the Bible. Just as no one is valueless, no one is godless in the true sense of the word. We all worship something. The well-known folk/rock songwriter and singer Bob Dylan penned a song in 1979 called "Gotta Serve Somebody." He was right.

We are all designed to worship something that we feel is worthy of our time and devotion. We were created to worship. The instinct is embedded in every one of us—the need to live for something outside of ourselves and bigger than we are. This has been true of every culture throughout human history.

In a recent interview with the magazine, The Hollywood Reporter, actress Jennifer Aniston made an honest statement that I believe many people can relate to. She is describing a longing that I believe can only and ultimately be satisfied by God:

> There's something bigger I'm interested in doing, It could be more work, it could be more creativity, or getting more

> philanthropic in the world. It can look like a baby. It can
> look like a foundation. I know I have a bigger purpose. It's
> a puzzle, and I haven't quite put the puzzle together. But
> something greater is calling out to me (Galloway, January
> 30, 2015).

Consider the many religions and cults. While most religions have a deity, or in many cases several deities, a foundation of almost every faith is becoming one with the universe or obtaining self-actualization. Rituals, chanting, time-consuming meditations, and even self-harm are all supposed to help bring the individual to ultimate realization. Some people accept reincarnation in hopes of reaching the highest plane of existence.

Many are trying to become one with the universe instead of becoming one with God. Many are trying to find their self-actualized purpose by looking within themselves instead of seeking their Creator, who has a destiny for all. God forbids non-Christian spiritual practices.

> There shall be not found among you anyone who makes
> his son or daughter pass through the fire, one who uses
> divination, one who practices witchcraft, or one who
> interprets omens, or a sorcerer, or one who casts a spell,
> or a medium, or a spiritist, one who calls up the dead. For
> whoever does these things is detestable to the Lord and …
> God will drive them out before you" (Deut. 18:10–12).

Séances, tarot cards, and Ouija boards are all forbidden according to the standard in this passage, since they will lead us away from our true purpose. All religions present a problem because they encourage us to find purpose through man-made efforts or demonic-inspired rituals while trying to explain our existence through experiences outside of ourselves. This becomes confusing. We cannot have it both ways.

The question is, what is it that we worship? Idleman says, "All of us are worshipers. Worship is hardwired in who we are. It's true of every culture and every civilization. Everyone worships" (Idleman 2013, 57). Jesus taught, "For where your treasure is, there will your heart be also" (Matt. 6:21). Our hearts may be attached to several things or individuals, like a spouse or our children. Whatever has the highest place in our hearts has the potential of being our god.

One of the Lord's most misunderstood statements addresses this truth. "He who loves father or mother more than Me is not worthy of Me; and he who loves son or daughter more than Me is not worthy of Me" (Matt. 10:37). Jesus was identifying two essential truths. First, there is no guarantee that any human being will not turn on you or betray you, while He will never leave you or forsake you (Matt. 28:20; Heb. 13:5). Second, no one else can provide the eternal security that Jesus can, so love for the Lord is essential for our eternal well-being. In the mind of the Hebrew of Jesus' day, the contrast was clear: though we have a natural love for family members, we are to love God more. Jesus was simply saying that our love for Him must supersede the love we have for anyone or anything else.

This leads us to our primary purpose. Whom or what do we worship and attach our lives to? Frangipane writes,

> One does not have to penetrate deeply into the Revelation of John to discover that both God and the devil are seeking worshippers (Rev. 14:7; 7:11; 13:4; 14:11). Time and time again the line is drawn between those who 'worship the beast and his image' and those who worship God" (Frangipane 2006, 89).

A true measure of our worship is what we do and whom we seek when life gets difficult and painful. "Someone once said that both God and the devil have a plan for our lives. And we are the ones who cast the deciding vote" (Larson 2013, 45). It is easy to worship God when everything is coming up roses. In fact, we may not feel the need to worship when life is going well. Our worship is tested, however, when tribulation and temptation arise.

When Job lost his servants, his children, his riches, and his health, his wife wanted him to "curse God and die" (Job 2:9). But Job had a much different response: "Shall we indeed accept good from God and not accept adversity?" (Job 2:10). Job continued,

> 'Naked I came from my mother's womb, and naked I shall return there. The Lord gave and the Lord has taken away. Blessed be the name of the Lord.' Through all this Job did not sin nor did he blame God (Job 1:21–22).

Our character is tested in hard times. Whom or what we worship clearly emerges when we have nothing else to depend on. Is it alcohol? Is it pornography? Is it prescription pills? Is it a boyfriend or a girlfriend? Is it a spouse? Is it self-absorbed pursuits? Or is it God? Our purpose depends upon our choices. Who we are and where we are going are determined by life's events and how we have responded to them.

We worship God because we know that we were created for His pleasure. "We were not created to live for ourselves, but for Him" (Frangipane 2006, 91). Do we not feel an overwhelming pleasure when we see our own children born? The same is true with God. He takes great pleasure in our lives and wants to see us enjoy His gifts. The Lord desires a people whose purpose for living is to please Him and to be a blessing to others. When He is pleased, we are pleased.

This is the feeling that Eric Liddell recognized, as I mentioned in chapter 1.

The first three commandments of Exodus 20 describe how the longing for purpose begins. First and foremost, we are to have no other gods beside the Lord God Almighty. Having no other gods sets the stage for many impartations, opportunities, and blessings throughout life. When we align our desires with God's purpose for us, we will see fulfillment. To show devotion to anything other than the Lord God of the Bible is to worship an idol and a false god.

When we worship and pursue a false god, our purpose in life will be hampered and often derailed. God loves us too much to want to see that occur. That is why He is described as a jealous God (Ex. 20:5; Deut. 4:24, 5:9; Jos. 24:19). Jealousy is not the same as envy. Envy is a sin. Jealousy says, "I have something I love. It is mine and may be threatened, hurt, or taken away, and I do not want to see that happen." Envy says, "You have something I want, and I desire to obtain it any way I can." The difference is ownership. God can't be envious, because He owns everything!

God does not want to lose us. God knows that as our life-giver, He is the only one who can lead us to our ordained purpose. Our purpose is directly related to our identity in Him. God says, "Bring my sons from afar and my daughters from the ends of the earth, everyone who is called by My name, and whom I have created for My glory" (Isa. 43:6–7). God knows that only through Him can any of us experience true fulfillment. He wants us to know that too.

Have you ever wondered why God hates idolatry so much? One reason is that He knows what we believe has power over us. Jennings writes, "Although we have power over what we believe, what we believe holds real power over us—power to heal and power to destroy" (Jennings 2013, 9). Therefore it is important to believe in the One who can give life and provide direction and purpose. Remember, we do not lead valueless or godless lives. Idleman asks a poignant question: "What if I told you that every sin you are struggling with, every discouragement you are dealing with, even the lack of purpose you're living with are because of idolatry?" (Idleman 2013, 12). By believing in and showing devotion to something, we give it permission to be our identity and to provide us direction and purpose, which in turn affects our behavior.

The first commandment is, "You shall have no other gods before me. You shall not make for yourselves a graven image [idol], or any likeness of what is in heaven above or on the earth beneath or in the water under the earth" (Ex. 20:3–4). God is making it clear that He is the one and only Creator and the one and only God. We are to worship Him and Him alone. God tells us this not because He has an ego complex but because He loves us. "The first and most important thing you could ever know about a relationship with God is that He set His affection upon you before you ever contributed anything to Him" (Wright 2005, 97).

Consider the people of Israel under Moses. While Moses was in God's presence for a short time (forty days), the people became restless. They became anxious about their leader and about their future. They worried about what was to become of them and about where they were going. They were an impatient people, and they looked for ways to do things themselves. When they felt God wasn't listening or wasn't quick enough to act on their behalf, they acted on their own. As a result, the people of Israel wanted to create a god in their own image. This was after just forty days!

What did they choose? Treat succinctly says,

> These people who saw the Red Sea divided made a calf to replace the God who delivered them! Not a bull! Not even

a cow! Not a lion! Not a tiger! A *calf!* A good-for-nothing calf! You can't milk or breed a calf. It's nothing! It's a calf! When men create their own gods, it's always good for nothing" (original emphasis) (Treat 1999, 39).

The Israelites, still fresh from living as slaves in Egypt for four hundred years, were familiar with the gods of Egypt, which were depicted as having the heads of animals and birds atop human bodies. Having been slaves, they must not have seen themselves as much more than a good-for-nothing calves. So they made a calf their god. This was what they wanted to reflect. As a result, their true purpose was diminished.

We may bow before the image of what we or someone else has created. God loves us so much that even though we fall short, He has made provision to redeem us to His image through Jesus. As people transformed in Christ, we are being restored to the image that God had in mind—His image! And with His image comes true purpose.

Hebrew, the original language of almost all of the Old Testament, uses several words for *idol*, and they are quite revealing. The most common word, *tselem*, means "resemblance," "a representative figure of," or "image." When we create an idol, it is a god in our image that we in turn reflect. Another word, *teraphim* (1 Sam. 15:23), means "a family idol" or "ancestor worship." The last two typical words for idol are interesting. One is *gillul* (2 Kings 23:24; 2 Chron. 15:8). This word means "a round figure," "a log," or "pellets of dung." The final Hebrew word used in the Old Testament is *eliyl*, which means "of no value," "good for nothing," or "no consideration."

These descriptions can help us see why God hates idols. He loves us so much that He wants us to have His name and His Image. He wants our purpose to be meaningful and to be aligned with His. His ways are not our ways. He desires the best for us and chose to redeem us when we fell to sin and brokenness. Our purpose does not rest upon idols. We have a much higher calling than that. Oh, how God longs for us to reflect Him rather than good-for-nothing pellets of dung!

In our fast-paced age, we are more impatient than the Israelites. We surely can't wait even forty days. We have a fast-food mentality and want things our way and now! We create gods that feed our selfish desires, and our purpose becomes wrapped up in what we have created. We will worship as long as we are benefiting, according to our plan, from the object of our worship. That is called shallow worship.

However, as soon as the pressures and disappointments of life arise, we rebel against the object of our devotion. Human nature makes us fair-weather friends. This is why we often see people changing habits, affections, and even churches at the drop of a hat. Such quick, impulsive changes can make us ineffective and can sabotage our purpose. What comes out of a person's heart during difficult times is a true measure of what is in him or her. When we expect God to do as we please, we will consider Him good only when He complies.

Isaiah 44:9–20 describes how people work hard at fashioning idols for themselves to worship, using the same materials that burn, gets consumed, and cook their food. Isaiah poignantly recounts the people saying to themselves, "I fall down before a block of wood!" (Isa. 44:19). Often, we work hard to build an idol of some kind, believing that it will provide hope and direction. We try to create something that will eventually give something back to us. How can something we create ever return the life we desire when we were the ones who gave the idol its existence in the first place?

Scriptures say, "Those who make them will become like them, everyone who trusts in them" (Ps. 115:8). People take on the characteristics of whatever they emulate. "What people revere, they resemble, either for ruin or restoration" (Beale 2008, 16). God created human beings in His image, but unfortunately, people often become more like the images they create and pursue. I don't know about you, but I would rather worship and serve a living, loving, and powerful God who can never be consumed or destroyed and who provides my identity and purpose than something made from a block of wood!

Many may say that civilized cultures do not worship wood-carved idols or goatlike images and so idolatry no longer exists. It is an ancient practice, the argument goes. What has not changed is that we will pursue someone or something beyond ourselves because we innately know we need more than what meets the eye to provide purpose in our lives. When we chase after something or someone, we often worship it. Idleman says,

> If you live in this world, then sooner or later you grow some assumptions concerning what your life is all about, what you should really be going after. And when you begin to align your life with that pursuit, then, whether you realize it or not, you are worshipping" (Idleman 2013, 59).

We all reflect what we worship. "The object of your worship will determine your future and define your life" (Idleman 2013, 60). We can see our purpose by observing what we are chasing.

To be in someone's image or likeness brings meaning and value to an individual. When a youngster hears that she is just like her mother or that he is the spitting image of his father, the connotation is usually a positive one. The youngster often feels a sense of belonging, value, and connectedness. When we understand that we are the images of our heavenly Father, it should encourage our connectedness to God and to His kingdom instead of to a kingdom of random chemical reactions. This understanding could lead to a distinct purpose for each of our lives.

If God breathed into us, then our lives did not occur by chance but by choice—His choice! The fact that we are living, breathing people means that we have a distinct purpose here on earth. We are not animalistic by nature, nor are we beings driven totally by sexual impulse, as Freud would have us believe. Rather, we are spirit beings first and foremost. God breathed life into all of us, providing a drive that can be based on value and purpose. We are created in the image of our Father, born on earth, and for a specific purpose.

Because of His love for His people, God through His prophets constantly admonished the Israelites of the Old Testament to destroy their idols. Much of the book of Isaiah speaks to the idolatry that had permeated the community of Israel. The prophet several times describes idols as lifeless, and he equates that lifelessness to Israel as well. For example:

> They will be turned back and will be utterly put to shame, who trust in idols, who say to molten images, 'You are our gods.' Hear, you deaf! And look you blind, that you may see … you have seen many things, but you do not observe them; your ears are open but none hears" (Isa. 42:17–18, 20).

The Lord knew that "they were becoming as spiritually lifeless as those gods, whom they erroneously thought had life" (Beale 2008, 69). Just as idols cannot see, speak, or hear, Israel became blind, foolish, and deaf. The people bowed down to gods that could not bring them life. As a result, the purpose they pursued was less than what it could have been had they remained faithful to the Lord.

We have created gods in many different forms. "We can only worship that which we know!" (Joyner 1993, 16). There are gods of food, gods of sports and entertainment, gods of romance and sex. Our boyfriend or girlfriend may become our god if he or she comes before the Lord. We have gods of achievement and success, gods of drugs and alcohol, gods of money, and ultimately the god of "me." Idleman asks,

> What enduring value has the god of wealth really bought anyone? Did the gods of pleasure ever once deliver true and lasting happiness? What about the gods of sex? Can they provide a joy that is more than that of a passing moment? What have these gods done for us? If anything, they have enslaved us. They have robbed us. They have disappointed us" (Idleman 2013, 66–67).

What we created will eventually place us in bondage. What we believe we have power over will begin to have power over us. This is the essence of any addiction. We chase all such gods for the purpose of happiness, but we experience the opposite instead.

The pursuit of happiness has become a god to many of us. Our country's Declaration of Independence, penned by Thomas Jefferson and signed by fifty-six delegates of the Continental Congress on July 4, 1776, says, "We hold these truths to be self-evident, that all men are created equal, that they are endowed by their Creator with certain unalienable Rights, that among these are Life, Liberty and the pursuit of Happiness." When we consider this declaration, we do not often mention life, and though we sometimes discuss liberty, we place the most attention on the pursuit of happiness.

Happiness can be mostly self-serving. Once in a while, we may feel happy when we observe someone else's pleasure. However, most of the time, we seek happiness through our own endeavors. I have spent time with many couples who are in conflict because one or both of them are no longer happy. Often, their happiness is based upon shallow considerations. Unrealistic expectations, self-centeredness, and lack of purpose are the three main reasons for unhappiness.

We often equate happiness with contentment. They are not the same. We can be happy without being content. Content people:

- Are more productive at their jobs.
- Typically have deep relationships with others.
- Help others and volunteer more.
- Are more likely to donate money to charity.
- Are more creative problem solvers.

And we can be content without feeling happy. Happiness is situational and circumstantially driven. We can be happy when we are eating. We can be happy when we win a game. We can be happy when we receive a compliment. We can be happy when we are at a party with friends. We can be happy when God answers prayer. We can also become unhappy very quickly. That's because happiness is fleeting. Three of the main things that will kill our happiness are:

- Comparing ourselves to others.
- A lack of close friendships.
- Holding on to resentments.

God desires our happiness, but His purpose is not to make us happy—it is to make us holy! Our purpose should be likewise—to be holy. To be holy means to be set apart, to be different, especially as it relates to the sinful, self-centered world. As we pursue the purpose of holiness, we gain more than happiness. After all, when we pursue our purpose we fulfill what is unique to us. We show that we are different from everyone else. We gain satisfaction, peace, and contentment. Indeed we gain life!

CHAPTER 4

Purpose: Sabbath Rest—Commandment Three

So there remains a Sabbath rest for the people of God ... strive to enter that rest.

—Heb. 4:9, 11

Be very careful, then, how you live—not as unwise but as wise, making the most of every opportunity, because the days are evil. Therefore do not be foolish, but understand what the Lord's will is.

—Eph. 5:15–17 (NIV)

We all want to be happy, entertained, filled, and pleasured. Our world is moving at great speed, and we want to enjoy life at the same pace. That comes at a cost, but we will pay whatever it takes to be happy more often and for the experience to last longer. Unfortunately, such drivenness is unsustainable and results in discouragement, depression, and breakdown. Our purpose becomes confused and derailed. The pursuit of happiness overpowers contentment, and we find little or no rest. We do not know how to recover. We do not take the time to rest and to recharge ourselves.

God designed us to be at rest regularly, but rest is foreign to our lifestyles. Our medical, emotional, and mental health take a beating, and we may experience physical exhaustion and breakdown. Many medical problems develop as a result, and they become a distraction to our purpose.

When we do not rest, we suffer many consequences and our purpose is effected. Sleep is increasingly recognized as important to public health, with sleep insufficiency linked to motor vehicle crashes, industrial disasters, and medical and other occupational errors (Institute of Medicine, 2006). Individuals who lack sleep are more likely to suffer from chronic diseases such as hypertension, diabetes, depression, and obesity as well as from cancer, increased mortality, and reduced quality of life and productivity (Institute of Medicine, 2006). The National Institutes of Health suggests that school-age children need at least ten hours of sleep daily; teens, nine to ten, and adults, seven to eight. However, because of demanding work schedules, twenty-four-hour television, and constant access to electronic technologies, most people get far less than they need to rest and be replenished.

So what is the answer? Does God have a plan to slow us down? He rested too, didn't He? What was that all about?

The Bible says, "And by the seventh day God completed His work which he had done; and He rested on the seventh day from all His work that he had done" (Gen. 2:2). You may ask, "Why would an omnipotent God need to rest after creating the universe?" God said, "Let there be …," and it was done. How much effort did that take? Those are fair questions, especially since elsewhere in the Bible we read that our Creator does not get weary (Isa. 40:28).

Genesis 2:3 says, "Then God blessed the seventh day, and sanctified it, because in it He rested from all his work which God created and made." The Hebrew word *shabath*, translated as "rest," does not refer to a requirement to sleep or to take a break due to weariness. Sabbath rest means, to cease regularly from and to enjoy the results of your work. It provides balance: "Six days you shall labor and do all your work, but the seventh day is a Sabbath to the Lord your God" (Exodus 20:9–10). In the vast majority of instances in the Bible, the word is translated as "stopping" or "ceasing" from work or a task. In only seven of sixty-eight instances is the word translated "rest" or "rested." Other Hebrew words are used to describe physical rest. For example, Exodus 23:12 says:

> Six days you are to do your work, but on the seventh day you shall cease [*shabath*] from labor in order that your ox and your donkey may rest [*nuach*], and the son of your female slave, as well as your stranger, may refresh [*naphash*] themselves. (emphasis mine)

The Hebrew word *sabbath* means "to cease." Just as God ceased from His creation work, we too are to cease from our day-to-day occupations and refocus on what's important. The Sabbath is a day to push the reset button. Taking a Sabbath rest is an act of faith; it's a reminder that no matter what we do, God is in control.

God liberated his people when they were slaves in Egypt, and in Deuteronomy 5:12–15, God ties the Sabbath to freedom from slavery. Anyone who overworks is really a slave. Anyone who cannot rest from work is a slave—to a need for success, to a materialistic culture, to exploitative employers, to parental expectations, or to all of the above. These slave masters will abuse you if you are not disciplined in the practice of Sabbath rest. Sabbath is a declaration of freedom.

When we cease from pursuing our material goals for one day each week, we're saying, "God, I trust You to maintain control while I spend this day focusing on You. I trust You to provide for my needs seven days a week even if I work on only six of them. Regardless of how much money I could earn today or how much remains on my to-do list from last week, today I'm going to rest my mind and my body and bask in Your presence."

The more we work, the less we focus on God. The more we are distracted, the less we acknowledge Him. (I will offer more on this in chapter 7). We are created to be in His presence, and we must rest to understand and to pursue our purpose.

Man was made in God's image—intended, as God's child, to reflect his Father. Since his Father worked creatively for six days and rested on the seventh, Adam, like a son, was to copy Him. Together, on the seventh day, they were to walk in the garden. That day was a time to learn all that the Father had to teach about the wonders of His creating work. Thus the Sabbath, according to Scottish theologian Sinclair Ferguson (2004), was meant to be father's Day every week. It was made for Adam and had a hint of the future in it. The Father had finished His work, but Adam had not. Adam needed to seek God and fellowship with Him for continued relationship, instruction, and peace.

However, Adam fell. He ruined everything, including the Sabbath. Instead of walking with God, he hid from Him (Gen. 3:8). It was the Sabbath, Father's Day, but God had to look for Adam! This context helps us to understand the significance of the fourth commandment. It was given to fallen man—that is why it contains a "you shall not." He was not to work but to rest. Externally, that meant ceasing from his ordinary tasks to meet with God. Internally, it involved ceasing from all self-sufficiency to rest in God's grace (Ferguson, 2004).

Considering this, what difference did the coming of Jesus make to the Sabbath day? In Christ crucified and risen, we find eternal rest (Matt. 11:28–30), and we are restored to communion with God (Matt. 11:25–30). The lost treasures of the Sabbath are restored. We rest in Christ from our labor of self-sufficiency, and we have access to the Father (Eph. 2:18). As we meet with Him, He shows us Himself, His ways, His world, His purpose, His glory (Ferguson, 2004).

The Bible says that the day of rest (Sabbath) is one of the main purposes of creation, set aside so God's people can break from the routine of work to contemplate Him. Jesus said the Sabbath was made for man, and not man for the Sabbath (Mark 2:27). So the Sabbath does not celebrate God's creation but celebrates God Himself. The Sabbath is a preview of heaven where we will cease from labor, striving, and languishing and will forever enter into God's rest. The author of the book of Hebrews encourages us to enter into that rest rather than fall into disobedience.

There is another aspect of rest as well. Genesis 2:3 is saying that God stopped creating after the sixth day—not that He needed to take a break. The Bible indicates how God felt about His work after He had ceased His creation. On several occasions, "God saw it was good" (Gen. 1:10, 12, 18, 21, 25). After human beings were created, God looked upon all His creation and declared "it was very good" (Gen. 1:31). God was able to rest because what He did was a direct extension of who He is! He is Creator, and when He completed His creation He ceased from His work. God did not just cease from His labor; He stopped and enjoyed what He had made. What does this mean for us? We need to stop to enjoy God, His creation, and the fruits of our labor.

When the Lord ceased from His work, He found rest in the expression of Himself—Creator. When creation was complete, God found pleasure in it. God's purpose is a direct manifestation of who He is. When God expresses who He is, He is at rest. Likewise, when we live out our purpose, we can be at rest. True rest is ceasing from labor, reflecting upon God's goodness to us, and enjoying the fruit of our labor when we know it is an expression of who we are.

Imagine being a musician who has just recorded a CD. After recording track after track, voice after voice, note after note, you cease work on the project. You place headphones over your ears and listen to the finished work. If you are satisfied, you lean back in your chair, take several deep breaths, and feel pleasure over your finished work. It is an expression of who you are and what you wanted to communicate in your music. Your restful sigh is a sign that you have completed something you are proud of and feel is an acceptable representation of who you are.

Incidentally, the Bible indicates that the seventh day is not closed. For all other days of creation, the Genesis text says, "There is the evening and the morning." There is no such closing for the seventh day. In the New Testament book of Hebrews, the author tells us to labor to enter into God's seventh day of rest (which is continuing). This is symbolic of the eternal rest of believers in Christ when we get to heaven. However, there is a present application as well. Hebrews 4:4, 11 says:

> For He has thus said somewhere concerning the seventh day, 'And God rested on the seventh day from all His works' … Let us therefore be diligent to enter that rest, lest anyone fall through following the same example of disobedience.

Rest can be a continuing experience in our lives. It is a lifestyle that eventually leads us into eternity. When we know our purpose and serve within it, we find rest. We work hard to achieve and to obtain. We must also make the effort to trust in God and to rest in Him. God's rest is discovering our purpose and pursuing it. God's rest is being with the Father through Jesus to worship Him and to hear from Him. Being in sync with God offers just a taste of the rest we will find when we reach heaven. In heaven, we will completely cease our labors and arrive at our purposed destination. In the meantime, we can experience some of that here on earth as long as we cease and spend time worshipping and thanking God, and staying in step with Him in order to experience what He has for us.

Finally, this day of devotion and rest is designed to ensure that we do not stray too far from God's pattern. The Sabbath can be a stabilizing anchor. If we focus on God on one out of every seven days, we are less likely to drift from Him. Our nation has changed since the middle 1970s and no longer offers a Sabbath. Stores, businesses, and banks were once typically closed on Sundays, and most families went to church together. As a result, our nation had an awareness of God. Most neighborhoods and relationships experienced peace and respect as a result.

Today, stores and businesses are often open seven days a week. Whether your tradition is to celebrate the Sabbath on Saturday or Sunday, the point is that we must keep it holy and set apart. Many people have jobs that require them to work on Sundays, not allowing for a Sabbath rest and contemplation. These people should take another day and rest and honor God with it. Their mental and physical health, as well as their spiritual health, is at stake.

Media have become extensive and intrusive, offering many distractions from the focus on God. We live on our cell phones; TV is always on—with hundreds of channels. We even require that church entertain us. The music is often too loud, distracting us from worship. What ever happened to resting in the presence of God? Contemplative prayer is a lost practice, viewed as being only for those who live in monasteries. As we have abandoned the Sabbath rest, we have pushed God further and further away from our consideration—if we think of Him at all.

Moments set aside for Bible reading and prayer in our public schools once provided a time of rest, during the school week. We have underestimated the difference that a small block of time made in the lives of our children. Think of the drastic change since prayer and Bible reading were declared unconstitutional and removed from public schools in 1963 by the US Supreme Court! Over the years, we have seen a gradual yet dramatic increase in turmoil, angst, conflict, resentment, disrespect, violence, unsettledness, and fear. People feel that they are being tossed around on a stormy sea. Many have lost their morals, ethics, honesty, and integrity—all because we are driven to take for ourselves instead of trusting in God and being at rest.

When our purpose becomes an extension of who we are in Christ, we will find that resting in who we are and what we do becomes easier and more satisfying. Our purpose, as well as our rest, begins with knowing Jesus as our Lord and Savior. When we do not know our purpose, we will often be tormented by the lack of peace and contentment. As a result, our lives may be spent striving only for happiness and self-seeking pleasures, and we will experience failure and disappointment.

Our foremost purpose is to worship God our Creator—to place Him first in our lives. In doing so, we may seem different and even weird to our contemporaries, but we will experience purpose that others crave. Once we commit ourselves to God through the saving power of Jesus, the Prince of Peace, we can discover the specific purpose He has for us here on earth. Then we can experience rest and contentment, since we will seek God, find Him, discover ourselves in Him, and be at rest. This is the "peace that passes all understanding" that Paul mentions in Philippians 4:7.

Thus the Sabbath is about more than rest for the body; it is about rest for the soul. We need rest from the anxiety and the strain of our overwork, which is really an attempt to justify ourselves—to gain the money or the status or the reputation we think we must have. Avoiding overwork requires deep rest in Christ's finished work for our salvation (Heb. 4:1–10). We must walk away regularly from our vocational work to obtain this rest.

The Sabbath is the key to getting this balance, and Jesus identifies himself as the Lord of the Sabbath (Mark 2:27–28)—the Lord of Rest! Jesus urges us,

> Come to me, all you who are weary and burdened, and I will give you rest. Take my yoke upon you and learn from me, for I am gentle and humble in heart, and you will find rest for your souls" (Matt. 11:28–29).

One of the Lord's great blessings is that He gives us rest that no one else will.

According to Ephesians 5:15–17, time management is a command. How we use our time determines our health, our contentment, our priorities, and our ability to have relationships. Dr. Tim Keller, the founding pastor of Redeemer Presbyterian Church in New York City, suggests some practical approaches to keeping the Sabbath.

First, take time for inactivity. This may sound like I am suggesting laziness. If that is your first thought, it says something about your lifestyle. However, filling your days with unplanned activities will not result in a true Sabbath. Rest and cessation of activities should be part of a Sabbath. Turning off the alarm clock and allowing the morning to ease into the day would be an example. God told the Israelites to let a field lie dormant every seven years (Lev. 25:1–7). The soil rested so overfarming would not deplete its nutrients and destroy its ability to keep producing.

Second, take time to do pleasurable things that can be inserted into your Sabbath. There is contemplative rest. Prayer, contemplation, and worship should be part of a Sabbath. As indicated above, even the ground needs a Sabbath. There is also recreational rest. Take a morning or afternoon jog or exercise class or do gardening. Then there is aesthetic rest. Take time to enjoy what is beautiful to you. Go bird watching, relax in a park or at the beach, or enjoy art or music.

Third, depending upon whether you are an introvert or an extrovert, choose time to be recharged accordingly. If you are an introvert, spend time someplace away from people and find replenishment there. If you are an extrovert, go to lunch or to the park with one person or a small group of dear friends and enjoy fellowship without an agenda. If what you do contradicts your temperament, it will not be a Sabbath for you.

Fourth, not all family time counts as Sabbath time. Parenting responsibilities never end, especially when children are young. Fun family time can be a part of the Sabbath, but try to maintain a balance and be sure that responsibilities are kept at a minimum. Parents may need a part of the day to be off and alone if possible. Family time can be spent in church or contemplating the reality of God in each family member's life. The key is to keep family time on a Sabbath in balance.

Finally, Sabbaths may be built around certain time frames and need not be just once a week. Vocations can be demanding, not allowing for weekly Sabbaths. Physicians in residency positions, first responders, pastors, teachers, and others have demanding jobs that require long hours. Be mindful of taking a sabbatical—a distinct time to be replenished and refreshed. In the nation of Israel, Sabbaths were observed every year to remember and to honor God. Leviticus 25:8–11 speaks of a year of Jubilee, observed on the fiftieth year in every cycle. Watch that you don't justify too little Sabbath by saying you're "going through a season"—when that season never ends.

If you must enter a season like this, it should not last longer than two or three years. Be accountable to someone for this, or you will get locked into an "under-Sabbathed" lifestyle and you will burn out. And during this under-Sabbathed time, do not let the rhythms of prayer, Bible study, and worship die. Be creative, but rest on your Sabbath.

Ultimately, the purpose of the Sabbath is not simply to rejuvenate yourself in order to produce more, nor is it the pursuit of pleasure. The purpose of the Sabbath is to enjoy your God, life in general, what you have accomplished in the world through His help, and the freedom you have in the gospel—the freedom from slavery to any material object or human expectation. The Sabbath is a sign of the hope that you have in the world to come.

As we grow in relationship with God and as we honor the Sabbath rest, we can grow in healthy relationships with one another. As we experience the purpose of loving the Lord our God with all our heart, soul, strength, and mind, we are then to love our neighbor as ourselves (Luke 10:27). To have good relationships with others, we need to have a meaningful relationship with God. Bad experiences in relationships with others can affect how we relate to God. The next two chapters address the qualities of purposeful relationships as declared by God in the Ten Commandments.

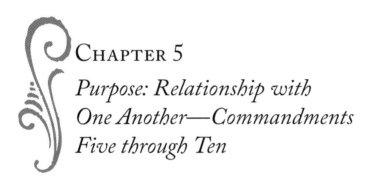

Chapter 5

Purpose: Relationship with One Another—Commandments Five through Ten

God loves people. He is not that interested in our bigness, wealth, popularity, or supremacy. He is interested in our relationship with Him and our relationship with people.

—Matthew Barnett (41)

For all that is in the world, the lust of the flesh and the lust of the eyes and the boastful pride of life, is not from the Father, but from the world.

—1 John 2:16

For you were called to freedom, brethren; only do not turn your freedom into an opportunity for the flesh, but through love serve one another.

—Gal. 5:13

We were created for relationships. Much of our purpose is revealed in the context of relationships. We are fulfilled and complete in them. Have you ever heard someone say about another that he or she "makes me complete"? Being in God's image means being relational. After all, as a triune God, He has been in relationship with Himself for eternity! We were designed not to be islands, because it is "not good for man to be alone" (Gen. 2:18).

Unlike most of the animal kingdom, human beings were created to reproduce within relationships and not simply for the sake of mating. Husbands and wives are to be together, raising their children. Husbands and wives are to experience love as it is expressed in a committed marriage relationship. So why is it that we are hurt most often in relationships? Human interactions are not always positive and loving. Many are abusive and destructive. Why is that? Six of the commandments can shed light on this. But let us begin at the beginning.

God commanded Adam and Eve to avoid the Tree of Knowledge of Good and Evil in the garden of Eden (Gen. 2:16–17). They were allowed to eat of any tree except that one. They could even eat from the Tree of Life. The Hebrew word *akal* means "to consume" or "to devour." According to the *American Heritage Dictionary*, to eat means to "to take in and absorb" and "to consume." *Webster's Dictionary* defines eating as "to bring into a specified condition by eating." When we eat and consume, we experience what we have eaten. We become full with it.

If Adam and Eve ate from the forbidden tree, they would experience good *and* evil and would be full of both! God's purpose was for human beings to avoid this tree. The restraints He imposed were for our benefit! We were meant for good, not evil. Relationship with God is the source of good and of all life. There was no such restrictions related to the Tree of Life. God did not want us to experience evil. The purpose for man and woman was to obey God and to enjoy complete, unbroken relationships and a fulfilled, unhindered personal destiny. God's intentions toward us were good from the beginning.

Adam knew the boundaries, and he also knew that crossing them would displease God. The Lord made it clear to Adam that evil and disobedience would lead to his death. Adam understood the difference between right and wrong, good and evil, and the consequences. Adam's knowledge of good came from God's righteousness in his life through relationship. Taking from the forbidden tree would cause Adam and Eve to determine for themselves what good and evil are, which leads to death. God's good leads to life. That is what God desires for us today – to know His righteousness, not try to determine our own.

The Hebrew word *yada* is used 944 times in the Old Testament with many nuances in its meaning. Its primary meaning is "to discern," "to recognize," and "to gain by experience." To know something intimately, one must experience it. When Adam "knew" Eve intimately (Gen. 4:1, 25); they had experienced each other sexually. So, to know evil, Adam and Eve would have had to experience it, and God's purpose was that they would not.

Knowing means to understand intimately through personal experience in increasing detail. Adam and Eve knew the difference between good and evil, but God was trying to protect their purpose— to know and to walk in His image, to love the God who created them out of love, to be fruitful and multiply, and to take dominion. God wanted Adam and Eve to multiply His righteousness on earth and to take dominion, using His attributes.

The Bible says, "The fear of the Lord is the beginning of knowledge" (Prov. 1:7) and "The fear of the Lord is the beginning of wisdom, and the knowledge of the Holy One is understanding" (Prov. 9:10). Notice that the foundation of knowledge and wisdom is honoring, obeying, and showing devotion to God—a loving God who desires our good and a wonderful purpose. He knew that if we experienced evil, everything would change. Evil came because Adam and Eve believed they knew better than God what was good for them. Evil comes today because we think we know better than God how to find our direction and purpose.

Sin is the experience of evil in one's life. God wanted no sin to contaminate Adam and Eve's purpose. God wanted to protect them from experiencing sin. For example, it is ludicrous to think that we need to have the experience of being a murderer, in order to *really* know that murder is evil. Satan lied to them by suggesting they would be like God if they experienced good and evil. They were already like God, since there is no evil in Him, and for a time, there was no evil in man or woman! Out of deception, envy, and self-centered ambition, Adam and Eve chose a path that led away from God and away from life. The same attitudes that caused Lucifer to be cast out of heaven caused humankind to be cast out of Eden and separated from God. The result was an altered purpose and destiny.

Envy is a powerful motivator. It is linked to Satan's weapons of doubt and distraction (see chapter 7). We want something that someone else has, believing that if we had it, we would be better people, more successful, and more acceptable. Sometimes we feel that we deserve to have what someone else has, because we would make better use of it than the other person does. That is called entitlement. We compare ourselves to others and what others have. We often use what others have to help define our purpose.

Once we compare ourselves to others, we derail our purpose. We attach ourselves to another person's purpose by wanting what he or she has and desiring to be like that person. Remember that when we create idols we become like them. The only person we are to become like is Jesus. He wants us to be like Him, because He knows that when we attach ourselves to Him, we find our identity and our purpose. "Sin of comparison bears only two kinds of fruit—pride and despair—neither of which come from the Vine [Jesus]," (Larson 2013, 41).

God's purpose for Adam and Eve suffered soon after the serpent's deception. Adam lied, or bore false witness, to God about who was responsible for the entire mess. First he blamed God for creating woman; then he blamed the woman. In fact, Adam was there during the conversation with Satan but did not rebuke the serpent or defend the Word of God (Gen. 3:6). Then, soon after Adam and Eve had their first two children—Cain and Abel—envy, coveting, and murder entered human history.

Murder

Life is essential for us to fulfill our purpose. That is why the Devil seeks to kill. Murder is defined as "the unlawful premeditated killing of one human being by another" (*Oxford* 2002, 889). The fifth commandment is straightforward: "You shall not commit murder." The first documented murder occurred when Cain killed his younger brother Abel, as recorded in Genesis 4. When someone is murdered, his or her purpose is snuffed out as well. The murderer also experiences an altered purpose as a result of the crime. God commanded us not to kill because He is the giver of life and because He knows that both victim and perpetrator have had their lives ruined.

However, Jesus raised the bar regarding this commandment. His standard probably puts us all in a place of conviction. He was dealing with the attitude of the heart, where the desire to kill originates, when He made this compelling statement:

You have heard that the ancients were told, "You shall not commit murder" and "Whoever commits murder shall be liable (guilty) before the court." But I say to you that everyone who is angry with his brother shall be guilty before the court; and whoever shall say to his brother, "Raca" (good for nothing), shall be guilty before the supreme court; and whoever shall say, "You fool" shall be guilty enough to go into fiery hell (parenthesis mine) (Matt.5:21–22).

General and constant putdowns, insults, and disparaging comments are in the same category as murder. Killing is more than ending a life. We can be guilty of murdering the character of another person. To Jesus, that sin also comes from a murderous heart. The apostle John added, "Everyone who hates his brother is a murderer; and you know that no murderer has eternal life abiding in him" (1 John 3:15). Often, a murderer has decided that another person's life is unworthy. Putdowns and insults over time will convince someone that such a devalued life no longer has purpose.

If a person believes that his or her own life no longer has purpose and hates that life, it often becomes easy for the person to hate someone else. Jesus said, "You shall love your neighbor as you love yourself" (Matt. 19:19). In the Greek language Jesus was saying that you shall love your neighbor insofar as you love yourself. We can give only what we have. If we hate ourselves, we will hate others. If we desire to harm ourselves, we will desire to harm others. If we are angry with ourselves, we will be especially angry with others. Consider how often we hear in the news about a person killing someone else or several others and then killing himself. On the other hand, when we feel good about ourselves, we will be good to others.

The murder rate in the United States for 2012—4.7 per 100,000 people—was significantly higher than in most other wealthy nations (www.rawstory.com/rs/2013/09/16). This figure came from a nation that was founded on biblical principles but has since drifted away from the things of God. The rate was 0.4 in Japan, 0.8 in Germany, 1.0 in Australia, 1.1 in France, and 1.2 in Britain, according to the Organization for Economic Cooperation and Development (www. rawstory.com/rs/2013/09/16). Among nations assessed by the Paris-based club of market economies, only Brazil, Estonia, Mexico, and Russia had higher murder rates than the United States.

Our purpose includes cherishing and protecting life. We have strayed far from the principles upon which our country was created. As soon as we as a nation no longer sanctified and protected life from conception, our attitudes about life in general deteriorated. Our purpose to protect life has become weakened. The vast majority of physicians are trained to do whatever they can to prolong life and to provide healing. They operate within the purpose of God as healers and life sustainers. The apostle Luke, who wrote the gospel that bears his name and the book of Acts, was a physician.

The majority of people seek to preserve life and often work in areas designed to better the life of their fellow man. Even those who do not work in the medical field are hard-wired to serve the common good. That is a huge part of our purpose and is manifested in countless ways. Life is to be cherished, but sin has lessened the importance of life for us. Protecting life brings blessings; ending life brings pain. This low view of life affects how we conduct relationships and our own care. The apostle Peter says:

> To sum it up, let all be harmonious, sympathetic, brotherly, kindhearted, and humble in spirit; not returning evil for evil, or insult for insult, but giving a blessing instead; for you were called for the very purpose that you might inherit a blessing (I Peter 3:8-9).

Adultery

Adultery is sexual activity with someone other than your spouse. Fornication, sex between unmarried people, also falls under this concept. This was understood throughout Israel in the Old Testament era. Adultery was a serious offense in the eyes of God and called for a serious sentence. The punishment was death (Lev. 20:10). During the times of the prophets, God used the term to describe the breach of Israel's relationship with Him through idolatry. God called idolatry "adultery" or "harlotry" because the people of Israel were unfaithful to Him (Ezek. 16:15).

In the New Testament, Paul equated friendship with the world with adultery because the union with Christ is broken by devotion to the things of the world (Rom. 7:4). Jesus spoke similarly, calling His contemporaries an "adulterous generation" (Matt. 12:39; 16:4).

Jesus condemned the transfer of affections from God to the world and from a spouse to another person, but He again raised the bar. He said, "You have heard that it was said, 'You shall not commit adultery'; but I say to you, that everyone that looks on a woman to lust for her has committed adultery with her already in his heart" (Matt. 5:27–28). Simply lusting after someone violates God's standard.

Pornography is a vice that fits this violation. Pornography is a combination of two Greek words: *porne,* which means "prostitute," and *graphein,* which means "writings." The "prostitute writings" industry takes in more than $15 billion every year (MyAddiction. com, 2013). Thirty million people in the United States alone log onto pornographic websites every day (MyAddiction.com, 2013). These people lust after an image. We have discussed how images that man creates are idolatry. Pornography is an "affair of the mind" that damages a marriage.

I have heard people try to justify the pursuit of pornography by saying, "I am not hurting anyone." That is a lie. It is a deception. The pursuit of pornography violates a marriage because it brings someone else into the relationship. This is adultery. In Matthew 5:21–22, Jesus identified the real issue. As with murder, adultery is a heart issue. Jesus declared, "For out of the heart come evil thoughts, murders, adulteries, fornications, thefts, false witness, slanders. These are the things which defile the man" (Matt. 15:19–20).

A large part of our purpose is faithfulness—especially regarding relationships. Faithfulness in anything, but especially relationships, is a critical component of our purpose. We are all called to be faithful in whatever we do. "If you have genuine faith, it will be exhibited by faithfulness. In other words, if I have faith in a faithful God, others will know it by the way that I live" (Briscoe 1991, 125).

The spirit of this commandment, therefore, is more than just keeping the marriage bed undefiled. It speaks to the heart of being faithful. "How can you claim faith in the living Christ, and being faithful to God, when you are living in unfaithfulness to your spouse?" (Briscoe 1991, 126). If we cheat in any area of life, we are not being faithful. Living according to God's purpose includes lining up our declared faith with a life of faithfulness. Briscoe writes:

> One of the tragedies of the church of Jesus Christ in the western world today is that we have made it so easy to 'believe' that we have put a great chasm between coming to faith and living faithful lives" (Briscoe 1991, 126).

Believing in Jesus and following Him are two different experiences. James 2:9 says that even demons believe. Our beliefs must be put to action. Following Christ is transformational! If we are not changing to be more Christlike, perhaps we are not truly following Jesus. Following Christ and His ways will lead us to our purpose.

If we know our purpose and await its fulfillment, are we being faithful to the Lord while we wait? Jesus affirmed the men who were faithful with what was given to them and who used it wisely. He said, "Well done, good and faithful servant! You have been faithful with a few things; I will put you in charge of many things" (Matt. 25:21, NIV). Often, if people are not faithful in their marriage, they are not faithful in other areas.

Are we remaining diligent until our time comes? Or are we falling into a trap like Abraham and his wife Sarah, as recounted in Genesis 15 and 16? They were given a promise toward a purpose by God, but after waiting years and becoming impatient, they decided to hurry God along and devised their own plan—which included adultery! Their lack of patience and trust in God caused tremendous conflict within their household. The "son of promise," Isaac, who represents Israel, was born about thirteen years after the "son of the flesh," Ishmael, who represents the Arab nations (Gen. 17, 18). The Middle East has been in conflict ever since.

If we do not yet know our purpose, are we seeking everything available to us except God? Are we asking Him to show us? Do we trust Him to show us? Are we being faithful to what we do know in the meantime? Faithfulness, or a lack thereof, will affect everyone around us and everything we do. Faithfulness is critical when pursuing our purpose. The spirit of this commandment is critical in our dealings with ourselves, with those we love, and with God.

Stealing

Stealing is taking for ourselves what does not belong to us. We may steal property; we may steal someone's affection; we may steal a position or title; we may steal an election to gain power. All stealing speaks to our unwillingness to wait and to trust God. It reflects the thief's rebellion and selfish ambition. It reflects pride, arrogance, and insensitivity. Ultimately, it is the Devil who is behind the desire to steal, for he himself came "to steal, kill, and destroy" (John 10:10).

The Federal Bureau of Investigation estimated that there were about nine million property crimes in 2012 (FBI.gov 2013). Stealing and murder are often linked. Victims of theft who try to protect what they own are often murdered. The Lord loves us and desires that we avoid taking from others. Proverbs says:

> They may say, "Come and join us. Let's hide and kill someone! Let's ambush the innocent! Let's swallow them alive as the grave swallows its victims. Though they are in the prime of life, they will go down into the pit of death. And the loot we'll get! We'll fill our houses with all kinds of things! Come on, throw in your lot with us; we'll split our loot with you." Don't go along with them, my child! Stay far away from their paths. They rush to commit crimes. They hurry to commit murder. When a bird sees a trap being set, it stays away. But not these people! They set an ambush for themselves; they booby-trap their own lives! Such is the fate of all who are greedy for gain. It ends up robbing them of life. (Prov. 1:11–19 NLT)

Stealing, ironically, robs us of life. It robs us of our purpose. When we take what belongs to someone else, we are usually motivated by envy, hatred, and greed. We may gain someone else's stuff, but we do not gain what really belongs to us. Jesus taught us not to be anxious for anything—food, drink, clothing, and our lives in general—because what can we possibly add by being anxious? "But seek first His kingdom and His righteousness, and all these things shall be added to you" (Matt. 6:25–34).

What belongs to us is given to us. We are stewards of everything we have. We crave significance and purpose, and we often gain them by selfish means. We do not need to steal. Something given or earned is much more meaningful and secure. God is a giving God. He has what we need. He is faithful in His promises. He knows our purpose. It is much better for us not to steal from others when God has something specifically in mind for us.

Lying

Our purpose is to live in truth. To bear false witness is to tell a lie. To tell a lie is to convey something that is not true. "Lying is a form of insanity. It denies reality and attempts to force others to deny the reality of a situation by manipulating their understanding of truth" (Hall 1996, 114). I have counseled individuals who, after living with the lies of their loved ones, began to believe they themselves were crazy. The constant lies eventually overwhelmed their ability to discern. That made it difficult to believe anything they sensed to be truth, thus breaking down their purpose.

The basis for any relationship is truth. Without truth there can be no trust. Part of our purpose is interfacing with others. Without truth and trust, our purpose to be in relationship is hindered. The Bible tells us:

> If we say that we have fellowship with Him and yet walk in the darkness, we lie and do not practice the truth; but if we walk in the light as He Himself is in the light, *we have fellowship with one another*, and the blood of Jesus His Son cleanses us from all sin (emphasis mine) (1 John 1:6–7).

When we lie, we often isolate ourselves in relationships. Lying keeps us separated. It keep us in darkness.

Lying also gives Satan entry to our lives. A person who lives a lie opens the door to spiritual oppression of himself and his family (Hall 1996, 114). Jesus describes a liar as being connected to Satan:

> You are of your father the devil, and you want to do the desires of your father. He was murderer from the beginning, and does not stand in the truth, because there is no truth in him. Whenever he speaks a lie, he speaks from his own nature; for he is a liar, and the father of lies" (John 8:44).

The longer we operate in darkness the more comfortable it feels. It gives us a false sense of safety, when in reality, we are in danger of altering our purpose in life.

Lying can be leaving things out of a story as well as adding them. "Lying also includes making exaggerated claims" (Comfort 1989, 124). We may lie about and embellish accomplishments on our résumé. Politicians have a reputation for lying through exaggeration and omission of the facts. Many people embellish a personal story to place themselves in a better light. Many will tell lies about their friends and relatives so that they themselves can come out smelling like roses. This is known as slander. Perjury involves taking an oath to tell the truth, only to lie in court. Proverbs 5:5 states, "A false witness will not go unpunished, and he who tells lies will not escape."

Paul lays out a description of evil, listing slander and gossip among the "big" sins. We need to realize that lying is a grave sin. He says,

> God gave them over to a depraved mind, to do those things which are not proper; being filled with all unrighteousness, wickedness, greed, evil, full of envy, murder, strife, *deceit*, malice, they are gossips, slanderers,

haters of God, insolent, arrogant, boastful, inventors of evil, disobedient to parents, without understanding, untrustworthy, unloving, unmerciful, and though they know the ordinance of God, that those who practice such things are worthy of death, they not only do the same, but also give hearty approval to those who practice them" (emphasis mine) (Rom. 1:28–32).

Lies develop a power of their own. If we believe a lie long enough, it feels like the truth. We then are deceived all the more. We may hear about a person from another who was offended and became resentful. The information is skewed and false, but the more we hear it, the more we believe it.

Another way lies develop power is the effort a lie requires to remain intact. Once a lie is told, we have to work hard to protect it. Additional lies are often required to support the lie, causing us to be quite creative. The emotional, mental, and spiritual energies this activity demands are draining. We become anxious and paranoid. I have spent many hours with individuals who have had their lives drained to the point where they were ready to change course. Often this was because of a false witness about themselves, about another person, or about an aspect of life. This is especially true of people engulfed in addictions. Keeping lies places us in bondage and derails us from our purpose.

When Jesus said that "the truth will set you free" (John 8:32), He was referring to the truth of the gospel. However, He was also speaking about truth in general. When we speak the truth, there is no need to hide, to embellish, to twist, or to waste energy keeping a lie in place. The truth is absolutely freeing. Anyone who has lived in lies and now speaks truth will attest to this. There is no bondage in telling the truth. Lying about anyone or anything will prevent freedom, hindering our purpose. Paul states this beautifully:

> Finally, brethren, whatever is true, whatever is honorable, whatever is right, whatever is pure, whatever is lovely, whatever is of good repute, if there is any excellence and if anything worthy of praise, let your mind dwell on these things" (Phil. 4:8).

Lusting or Coveting

Just as we may lust after another person, we can lust after material things. Both lead to a desire for something that does not belong to us. The desire for someone else's stuff often leads to stealing. Before we get to the point of wanting another person's possessions, a motivation emerges within us. It is called envy. This is the feeling that we are being overlooked, ignored, and not having our needs met. "The love of God ceases to operate through us when envy has its way in us" (Larson 2013, 44). Envy arises especially when we compare ourselves with others and perceive that we have come up short. There is no need for envy. The kingdom of God is vast enough for all of us to have a purpose.

Coveting occurs when envy leads us to devise a plan to take what we feel we should have. Coveting is wanting something for the wrong reasons. The Bible says, "For where jealousy and selfish ambition exist, there is disorder and every evil thing" (James 3:16).

When we believe we have come up short, especially in our competitive society, we may develop a feeling of entitlement. Someone has what we think we should have, so we consider ways of getting it from that person. Our focus is on what others may have, and this diverts our attention from God. As long as we play the comparison and entitlement game, we will not be satisfied and we will be distracted from discovering our purpose.

We may feel a little discouraged about our marital relationship and covet someone else's spouse. Pornography and affairs may result from such covetousness. The last two of the Ten Commandments address the material positions of others and people related to another, such as wives. One important distinction to keep in mind: lust seeks to get; love seeks to give!

God is a giving God. Everyone seems to know John 3:16. If we sliced that verse into a shortened form—"For God so loved the world, that He gave"—we would still have the essence of the gospel. As creatures made in His image, we are designed to give as well. A huge part of our purpose is to give for the good of others. Think about all the types of work that human beings do. Most of them involve providing goods or services for the improvement of life. That is giving to others. Envy and coveting are totally contrary to a giving motivation. They perfectly describe Satan's nature. Remember that he seeks to "steal, kill, and destroy"—all taking activities. Satan is a taker; God is a giver.

There is great satisfaction when we work for and serve others—and, of course, great gain. Even if we have our own business, we serve and supply our customers. Our work matters to God. More important, our attitudes about work and serving others matter to God. One of my students wrote,

> I used to think that I worked to help support our family, and even though that is true, I found that God had other uses for me there. Until I matured as a Christian and started asking God to use me in my job for His glory, then I saw things differently. Since I have opened myself up to God's will in my work, amazing things have happened. I have been able to share with co-workers and see healing in their lives. God has blessed my income since giving my job to Him. I had always struggled and was never happy when I tried to earn more at work on my own, and my attitude was negative because of it. I never felt what I did was ever good enough for anyone, and I was unhappy. Now that my

heart is set right about my work, I am very fulfilled and happy, and I am able to be a good example to my family and co-workers.

Christian workers especially have a basis for doing their jobs out of love for mankind and not just to make ends meet (Sherman and Hendricks 1987). Our attitudes can be rewarding to us as well. Consider these biblical verses.

- "Lazy hands make for poverty, but diligent hands bring wealth" (Prov. 10:4 NIV).
- "Lazy people want much but get little, but those who work hard will prosper" (Prov. 13:4 NLT).
- "Do not love sleep, or you will become poor; open your eyes, and you will be satisfied with food" (Prov. 20:13).
- "Do you see a man skilled in his work? He will stand before kings; he will not stand before obscure men" (Prov. 22:29).
- "Diligent hands will rule, but laziness ends in forced labor" (Prov. 12:24 NIV).
- "Those who work their land will have abundant food, but those who chase fantasies will have their fill of poverty" (Prov. 28:19 NIV).
- "Whatever your hand finds to do, verily do it with all your might" (Eccl. 9:10).
- "Do not work for the food which perishes, but for the food which endures to eternal life, which the Son of Man shall give to you" (John 6:27).
- "Do all things without grumbling or disputing; that you may prove yourselves to be blameless and innocent, children of God above reproach in the midst of a crooked and perverse

generation, among whom you appear as lights in the world"
(Phil. 2:14–15).

- "For even when we were with you, this we commanded you,
that if any would not work, neither should he eat" (2 Thess.
3:10 KJV).

These verses and many more convey the idea that we are not
created to be idle or selfish. We are created to be fruitful with a
purpose and to achieve contentment.

Conclusion

Our lives are not lived in a vacuum. We are created to be in
community. God said it is not good for man to be alone. He wanted
human beings to realize the value of working together for the common
good, thus reflecting the love of the Father for His creation. Our
purpose is to be stewards of God's creation and to be ambassadors of His
love to others. I am not referring to welfare; I am referring to working
together. I am not referring to handouts to those unwilling to work;
I am referring to the mutual benefits of productivity, prosperity, and
generosity. When we choose to follow God's ways, we will experience
His pleasure and the betterment of our fellow human beings.

Every choice has a consequence—good or bad. Significant choices
have significant consequences. Our choices affect others. There is no
denying that. Our purpose includes how we interact with others.
Whom we love, how we love, how we work, whom we honor, all lead
to how we discover and fulfill our purpose. Rice says,

> Along with the capacity to make significant choices,
> in particular to choose whether or not to accept God's
> love, God also granted the creatures the capacity to love
> one another, to interact with and influence each other
> in profoundly significant ways. It is one of life's great

privileges to contribute to the lives of other people and to receive their contributions to ours. A world where people are genuinely affected by what others decide and do is also a world where people can do each other harm" (Rice 2014, 49).

God's commandments help us understand what will bring us rewards and contentment. His ways provide us with our purpose. In Romans 7:7, Paul says,

What shall we say then? Is the Law sin? May it never be! On the contrary, I would not have come to know sin except through the Law; for I would not have known coveting if the Law had not said, "You shall not covet."

Just as in the Garden of Eden, God's ways restrain us from evil and harm. Human nature compels us to seek after our desires without constraints. We would do well to understand that God's constraints are for our good and for our peace. He is much like a parent reining in a child. His intent is to help us develop healthy ways to meet our needs by doing what is right.

Our purpose is to seek God to receive what He has for us, not to seek what He has given to others. What He has given to others is for their purpose. He has a purpose in store for everyone. We should not take for ourselves. If we seek God, He will give to us.

This well-known passage offers a helpful reminder:

Do not be anxious then, saying, "What shall we eat?" or "What shall we drink" or "With what shall we clothe ourselves?" For all these things the gentiles eagerly seek; for your heavenly Father knows that you need all these things. But seek first His kingdom and His righteousness; and all these things shall be added to you (Matt. 6:31–33).

Our purpose is directly tied to how we treat the men, women, and children in our lives. Our purpose is to bring life, nurturing, help, and encouragement to others. Our purpose is to have a good work ethic and to be fruitful, since this not only helps us provide for our families but also benefits the common good. Our purpose is to be faithful in our relationships, especially in marriage—not to pursue sexual images and fantasies that bring distance and heartbreak to those we love and who love us.

Our purpose is to seek God for our desires and provisions and to be content with what we have. It is not our purpose to be selfish and to take what does not belong to us. It is not our purpose to be envious of what others have but to seek God for what is good for us. He surely knows us better than we know ourselves. Our purpose is to be free from the bondage of lies and freed in the truth so that we can be trustworthy.

Consider Paul's letter to the Thessalonians.

> Finally then, brethren, we request and exhort you in the Lord Jesus, that, as you received from us instruction as to how you ought to walk and please God (just as you actually do walk), that you may excel still more. For you know what commandments we gave you by the authority of the Lord Jesus. For this is the will of God, your sanctification; that is, that you abstain from sexual immorality; that each of you know how to possess his own vessel in sanctification and honor, not in lustful passion, like the Gentiles who do not know God; and that no man transgress and defraud his brother in the matter because the Lord is the avenger in all these things, just as we also told you before and solemnly warned you. For God has not called us for the purpose of impurity, but in sanctification. Consequently, he who rejects this is not rejecting man but the God who gives His Holy Spirit to you. Now as to the love of the brethren ... we urge you brethren, to excel still more, and make it your ambition

> to lead a quiet life and attend to your own business and work with your hands, just as we commanded you; so that you may behave properly toward outsiders and not be in any need. (1 Thess. 4:1–12)

These are the desires of God for our lives as represented in many of the Ten Commandments. However, since human beings are broken and sinful by nature, we all need to be redeemed. Our ability to live with purpose and according to God's blueprint depends upon our transformation from darkness into light. Luke 6:45 alludes to this truth:

> The good man out of the good treasure of his heart brings forth what is good; and the evil man out of the evil treasure brings forth what is evil; for his mouth speaks from that which fills his heart.

The success of our purpose hinges upon our surrender to God and His redeeming power, our willingness to follow His ways, our faithfulness to God, and how we treat our fellow human beings. Proverbs 6:22–23 describes the law of God this way:

> When you walk, they will guide you; when you sleep, they will watch over you; when you awake, they will speak to you. For these commands are a lamp, this teaching is a light, and the corrections of discipline are the way to life. (NIV)

There is one more commandment to discuss. It clearly brings a promise toward the fulfillment of our purpose.

CHAPTER 6

A Purpose with a Promise: Commandment Four

My son, observe the commandment of your father, and do not forsake the teaching of your mother.
> —Prov. 6:20

Honor your father and your mother, as the Lord your God has commanded you, that your days may be prolonged, and that it may go well with you on the land which the Lord your God gives you.
> —Deut. 5:16

The family has been the essential unit of every society since the beginning of time. This was God's idea. He established the family through a man and a woman at the very beginning. Every community is founded upon the family. "If the integrity of the family is destroyed, then the cohesion that binds towns, cities, and nations begins to disintegrate" (Robertson 2004, 118). Our society has witnessed this phenomenon. As the family unit breaks down, so does the security of the culture. Absent and abusive parents have not only hurt their children but have had a ripple effect on society. Substance abuse, depression, domestic abuse, and sexual promiscuity are among the many dysfunctions resulting from less-than-ideal parenting. They have caused a chain reaction in the world around us.

On the other hand, there is a growing sentiment to question authority, and it usually begins with dishonoring parents. "Though the family has long been the primary building block on which our society has grown strong, most recently, the authority of parents has been undermined" (Robertson 2004, 123). The wisdom of our time has blamed our parents for all of our ailments and pathologies. Our environment has a heavy impact on how we view God, ourselves, and the world. However, the way we respond to our environment has as much, if not more, of an impact upon our worldview and decision-making. We are responsible for our attitudes, choices, and actions.

When we consider our parents, we notice that they are imperfect. However, so are we! We will be imperfect parents as well. This is not terribly profound, but it is true. Mistakes were and will be made. Most mistakes are not life-altering, but some are grievous. That is the result of the fall in the garden of Eden. But parents are still life-givers and still love their children. "However much the divine image may have suffered from sin and unbelief, certain vestiges remain; chief among them is the love of the parent for the child" (Rosenbaum 1994, 106).

God has given parents their position. Parents are an extension of His authority. One day we may have the same honored position. Like any other purpose, it is a privilege and not a right. To help raise and nurture the next generation is a privilege. Parents are not called to raise children—they are called to raise adults! Parents are called to a high purpose: to prepare young people to be productive contributors to their own future families and to the common good.

In a minority of cases involving the extremely deviant parent, one could say the love for their children did not exist. But most parents love their children, want the best for them, try to guide and protect them, and seek to launch them into healthy and positive lifestyles. Christian parents also want their children to honor and serve God in the decisions they make.

Parenting is the hardest job in the world (with single parents having the toughest challenge). Parents often labor behind the scenes for the sake of their children. And children do not always notice what parents do for them. Parenting is an inglorious job, a self-sacrificing endeavor to be sure.

As we grow up, human nature emerges. We begin to recall the mistakes, the discipline from parents, the passing remarks, the insensitive moments, the forgotten promises, and the restrictions laid upon us with the words *wait* or *no*. These memories often remain foremost in our minds, and we fail to recognize the love our parents showed. We tend to ignore or to overlook the motivation of love behind a parent's actions. As we recall unhappy moments, we grow more distant and accusatory of our parents. We forget who our parents really are to us—life-givers! Often, the guidance they offered was intended to prevent us from going astray.

As a teenager, I chafed over letting my parents know where I was when I was out with friends. They required me to call when my location changed from where they first knew I would be and when I might be late arriving home. I noticed several of my peers did not have to do that, so I thought, *Why should I?* The situation produced many a conflict, and I often felt embarrassed, controlled, and cramped.

I have come to realize, especially after becoming a parent myself, that love and a desire for my safety motivated my parents' request.

It wasn't about control at all. By imposing this requirement, my parents also taught me how to be considerate of others, especially of the ones I love. They wanted to know I was safe, and by calling, I showed consideration for people who loved me. I understood that when I eventually wanted the same for my own children. Many other examples of how I ignored or misinterpreted my parents' intentions come to my mind. If you are honest, I know you will recall many from your own family.

No can be one of the most loving words parents have at their disposal. In the beginning of human history, God used the word when He mentioned the forbidden tree. The concept of "no" was acceptable to Adam and Eve until someone came along to challenge it, making God look like the kind of parent He was not. God was seen as a killjoy, as a withholding and controlling figure.

Adam and Eve placed themselves under a curse by disobeying their heavenly Father. Conflict and separation resulted. Their decision dramatically altered their purpose! "A child with a broken relationship is under a curse. He has violated the first commandment with a promise, whether he knows it or not, and it cannot be well with him" (Rosenbaum 1994, 108). The same conflict has continued ever since and has become even more contentious today. "Nothing is more common in our culture than people who have given up on their parents" (Rosenbaum 1994, 64).

Many young people, and many adults as well, resent their parents and feel that mom and dad cramp their style. But parents see more, know more, and have experienced more than their children. "They have learned more from their own mistakes than you have, and they have been gifted by God with special insight into the real needs of their children" (Rosenbaum 1994, 31). The truth is that most parents love their children and want the best for them. Children do not believe this truth often enough. Someday they may realize that their parents' love for them was greater than they ever knew.

The only commandment with a promise attached to it is the fourth commandment: "Honor your father and your mother, that your days may be prolonged in the land which the Lord your God gives you" (Ex. 20:12). This has been one of the most used and misused commandments, quoted by religious and nonreligious people alike.

Honoring your parents is not just an Old Testament concept. Jesus teaches this commandment in three of the four gospels (Matt. 15:4, 19:19; Mark 7:10, 10:19; Luke 18:20). More important, Jesus modeled honoring His own earthly mother. When He was suffering on the cross – *on the cross* – He commanded John, the one disciple who was there, to care for His mother. Joseph had died some time before Jesus' crucifixion, leaving His mother Mary a widow. From the cross, while dying in excruciating pain, Jesus declared to John, "'Behold your mother!' And from that hour the disciple took her into his own household" (John 19:27).

Paul teaches in Ephesians 6:2–3, "Honor your father and mother (which is the first commandment with a promise), that it may be well with you, and that you may live long on the earth." Paul adds a powerful phrase that echoes part of the Old Testament promise: "that it may be well with you." These words are found nowhere else in the New Testament.

Ephesians 6 is well known as a chapter that deals with spiritual warfare. "If you want to be strong in spiritual warfare, take time to consider the beginning of the chapter" (Rosenbaum 1994, 10). The second part of Ephesians 6 deals with the armor of God and combating the wiles of the Devil. The first few verses of the chapter deal with family relationships. I have spent time with many people who know what it is like to be in broken relationships. It is a spiritual dynamic.

The Devil is particularly adept at disrupting families, where spiritual warfare begins. If he convinces us that our parents are too controlling, don't understand us, are out to get us, or not operating out of love, we develop thoughts and behaviors that dishonor them. If we dishonor our parents, the first authority in our lives, we will have trouble with any other authority that comes our way, including God. Our parents are given to us to help us discover our identity and our purpose. Good parents see our talents and tendencies and are committed to guiding us and helping us. Good parents don't dictate our destiny but should speak what they see and encourage us toward our God-given calling.

When the commandment with a promise is broken, "it is well with you" becomes a personal issue. It is not by accident that this commandment is listed right after the command to honor God and before the commandments that deal with how to relate to others. Piety and the love for God also hinge upon how we honor our parents. Consider Deuteronomy 27:15–26:

> Cursed is the man who makes an idol or a molten image, an abomination to the Lord, the work of the hands of the craftsman, and sets it up in secret, and all the people shall answer and say, Amen. Cursed is he who dishonors his father or mother, and all the people shall say, Amen. Cursed is he who moves his neighbor's boundary mark … Cursed is he who misleads a blind person on the road … Cursed is he who distorts the justice due an alien, orphan, and widow … Cursed is he who lies with his father's wife … Cursed is he who lies with any animal … Cursed is he who lies with his sister, the daughter of his father or of his mother … Cursed is he who lies with his mother-in-law … Cursed is he who strikes his neighbor in secret … Cursed is he who accepts a bribe to strike down an

innocent person … Cursed is he who does not conform
the words of this law by doing them.

Notice how these are in similar order to the Ten Commandments!
First, honor God; then honor parents; then be in right relationship
with others. Cursed is the person who does not abide by the law.
"The emphasis is strong: *before you worry about stealing, cruelty, or
sexual sins, you should worry about dishonoring your parents.* Failure to
keep the first commandment with a promise makes it harder to keep
the commandments that follow it" (original emphasis) (Rosenbaum
1994, 28).

Why is this so important? Parents are our life-givers! Ultimately,
God is our life-giver. If we honor one, we honor the other. If we
do not honor our life-givers, we will not honor our purpose in life.
We may not find our purpose in life. We may be miserable in that
purpose. Aspects of our purpose will be less than pleasant. If we
do not honor our parents, we usually do not honor God with our
lives. Honoring God, then our parents, enhances our opportunity
to discover and fulfill our purpose in life. One of my clients wrote:

> I am independent, a leader, excellent at getting things done
> and taking care of myself, as well as those around me. This
> did not always make life easy. Mixing my personality with
> being a teenager caused many conflicts with my parents.
> I was disrespectful at times and thought I knew what was
> best for my life. Ever since that rocky time in my life I have
> done my best to make sure that I am living with the right
> priorities and being the me I want to be. Through those
> years of maturity I can look back at that time and while
> regretting the way I treated my parents, I am thankful for
> their continued love and firm guidance in my life. I am so
> very blessed that the Lord allowed that time to develop
> me for the better and helped me find my identity in Him.

When you do not honor God or your parents, you will not honor others. This is a heart issue. "Outward obedience coupled with inward rebellion could bring only a curse into your life, not a blessing" (Rosenbaum 1994, 117). In this circumstance, you can bet that you will not find your purpose, nor will business, health, finances, and relationships "be well with you."

The confusion, and often the argument, usually center on the meaning of honoring one's parents. What does it mean to do this? The Old Testament primarily uses three words rendered as *honor*: *kabed*, meaning "heavy," "weighty," "highly valued and esteemed"; *hadar*, meaning "to swell up," "to favor," or "to give honor and glory to"; and *yeqar*, meaning "costliness," "precious," and "dignity." Harris, Archer, and Waltke put honor in clear perspective:

> Persons in positions of responsibility and authority were deserving of honor (Ex. 20:12; Mal. 1:6). It is significant to remind oneself that giving honor or glory is to say that someone is deserving of respect, attention and obedience. A life which does not back up one's honorable words is hypocrisy of a high form. Israel was again and again guilty of honoring God with her lips, while by her actions making Him appear worthless (Isa. 29:13). (Harris et al., 1980, 427).

We may say we honor our parents, but we often treat them as being worthless. We will reap what we sow. That is a law of the universe established by God from the beginning.

The New Testament primarily uses two Greek words rendered as *honor*. The word *timao* means "to value" and to "esteem highly." What do we value? Do we value things over relationships? Self-centered behavior over giving to others? "God's idea of 'value' and ours, no doubt, are poles apart" (Comfort 1989, 122). The word *doxazo* means "to glorify," "to compliment," or "to magnify." An additional concept in the biblical language is to "do what is right when asked."

Paul writes about parents in several of his letters. In Ephesians 6:1, he prefaces the commandment by saying, "Children, obey your parents in the Lord, for this is right." Colossians 3:20 says, "Children, be obedient to your parents in all things, for this is well-pleasing to the Lord." Old and New Testament writers do not provide an age distinction. Change occurs when children marry. The spirit of the commandment remains the same—to respect and highly esteem one's parents.

Proverbs has twelve verses related to parents. They all have the same spirit and carry the same instruction. For example:

- "Hear, my son, your father's instruction, and do not forsake your mother's teaching; indeed they are a graceful wreath to you head, and ornaments about your neck" (Prov. 1:8–9).
- "A fool rejects his father's discipline, but he who regards reproof is prudent" (Prov. 15:5).
- "He who curses his father or his mother, his lamp will go out in time of darkness" (Prov. 28:24).
- "Listen to your father who begot you, and do not despise your mother when she is old" (Prov. 23:22).

The way we honor our parents undergoes a transition from childhood to adulthood and then again when we develop our own household with a spouse and children. We should honor and obey our parents unless they tell us to break the Ten Commandments or any other part of God's law. For example, if our parents tell us to have an abortion, we should not obey them, for that is killing a child. If we are told by our parents to steal from someone or to rob a bank, we should not obey them. Parents should not force a child to lie for them to an employer, a family member, or any other person.

Children and young people sometimes face serious and difficult threats, such as incest and physical abuse. Those situations are covered by the laws of God, found in Leviticus and Deuteronomy, and young people must ask another adult whom they trust to report the parent to the authorities ASAP in order to protect themselves. These are gross and grievous violations of God's law. Therefore obedience is not required.

The requirement to obey our parents also changes when we become adults with our own families, though we must still honor them. "At marriage the husband assumes the leadership of a new household. The new household is pursuing their own purpose and vision. How can he 'know … how to rule his own house' (1 Tim. 3:5) unless he is free from his parents' authority?" (Rosenbaum 1994, 126). The husband now stands before God, not his parents. The husband, not the wife's father, is now the head of her family.

A married person has four parents to honor if they are still living. Parents may still be a resource if direction is needed, and so they are to be valued and respected. Spouses should not suggest cutting ties with parents. Such actions can lead to a situation where things do not "go well for you."

Another time where "our duty to God may overrule the first commandment with promise" (Rosenbaum 1994, 124) is when we are obeying the call of God for our life. This can get sticky. We are not to use "hearing from God" as a way to disobey or dishonor our parents. That can be an easy copout. Parents may be in a unique position to confirm what God is saying to their children. If we are not married and if God has indeed spoken to us, it may be that we are to wait until our parents hear from God regarding the issue. Parents have the responsibility to assist and encourage our destiny, so it behooves us to accept their support.

On the other hand, there may be times when we have heard from God regarding our purpose and destiny, and our parents are unsupportive, envious, or outright destructive when we try to fulfill our calling. However, turning eighteen or twenty-one does not automatically release us from obeying our parents. Those may be the ages given by society, but the Scriptures cite no age of release concerning obedience to our parents. Even King David and Jesus remained subject to their parents in their youth and through early adulthood. Our calling will be our calling, even if it occurs later than we had anticipated and desired. When this happens, it may be essential for us to heed the wait. Waiting on God is a common topic in the Scriptures. God often uses delay to mature us so that when it is time for our purpose, we will be ready. Our calling is in God's hands, and He can overcome any obstacle.

Some may be saying right now, "What about abusive, addicted, overbearing, neglectful, and absent parents?" These are real considerations, since more and more young people are experiencing such parental issues. But many young people react to parents' anger by calling it abuse, when in fact a young person's behavior or attitude has dishonored his or her parents. Parents have every right to correct their children. However, anger can lead to abuse. "We should not leave home because a parent is angry with us. But we should leave when our lives are in danger" (Rosenbaum 1994, 54).

The increase in divorce has brought many challenges for those affected. Divorce has a tremendous negative effect upon people, especially children. Our culture has grossly underestimated the impact of divorce upon the individuals involved, the family unit, and society as a whole.

If only one parent is present in the home and available, he or she is probably working very hard to provide for and nurture the children. The child or young person should all the more honor and obey that parent, because the parent is laying down his or her life for the child. If possible, a young person should seek communication and relationship with the absent parent. If that is not possible, a child often feels a sense of loss and hurt and may need other nurturing adults to help fill the gaps. Extended family plays an important part in the life of such a child. Perhaps church life and counseling are needed. Most important, relationship with Jesus and the healing power of a loving God can help children know that they are valued and that their heavenly Father will never leave them (Matt. 28:20; Heb. 13:5; Ezra 9:9).

Before David became king, he was married into a family whose father, King Saul, was out to kill him. Not the most secure environment! Yet, while Saul showed envy and hatred for his son-in-law, David never dishonored him. On three occasions, David had the chance to kill Saul and to remove the threat on his life. Yet he spared the king each time, because he honored God and God's anointed authority. I encourage you to read 1 Samuel 24:2–22, a poignant account of the outcome of David's approach to his father-in-law.

David also showed kindness to Saul as he ministered to him through music, calming the anxiety and turmoil within the king. David looked for ways to love Saul. "Unlike many of us, he did not cut off communication. No, he looked for opportunities to appeal to Saul's better nature" (Rosenbaum 1994, 55). Hall adds:

> Honoring their father doesn't mean children put up with abuse or keep quiet about how much they're hurting. Honoring their father means they treat him like a man instead of a child. A man can take what other people

think about him, a child cannot. But when the children tell him what they think of his behavior, they must do it with honor for his position as their father and as a human being" (Hall 1996, 127).

Finally, after Saul died in battle, David mourned over the loss, even though he knew he was to directly benefit from Saul's death. David remained confident in his purpose, and as a result, he was able to treat Saul with honor and not with contentiousness or disdain.

Noah had just completed an ocean journey for the ages (Gen. 7–8). He and his three sons built an ark and stored away food for the many animals aboard. He witnessed a flood that was unleashed upon all the earth. Noah and his family remained faithful to their purpose as directed by God. He landed upon dry ground as the waters receded and decided to drink a lot of wine (Gen. 9:21). He became drunk and apparently lost his faculties, stripping himself naked. His sons happened to come upon him in two different shifts, with two very different outcomes.

One son, Ham, dishonored his drunken father, while his other two sons, Shem and Japheth, showed respect (Gen. 9:22–29). Despite the embarrassment of seeing their dad naked and two sheets to the wind, they acted with care and grace toward him. As a result, Ham and his son, Canaan, were cursed while Shem and Japheth were blessed. Even when a parent is behaving in a dishonorable manner, a child is accountable for his or her response to the parent.

After my mother died when I was seventeen years old, my father's drinking problem became worse. There were many times when he would pick a fight with others during a group gathering, and I would feel quite embarrassed. Many of those times, I simply talked Dad into taking my brother and me home. I sometimes did the driving. Removing my dad from potentially volatile situations was embarrassing, frustrating, and disappointing. There were times when he would come after me over little things and would even attempt to provoke a fistfight. I never laid a hand on my dad and learned how to de-escalate these situations. Sure I was angry, and I voiced my frustration loudly at times, but I tried not to dishonor my father. Often, the next day it was as if nothing ever happened, which could also be frustrating. The relationship remained intact, albeit strained at times.

My father died when I was in my early thirties, and for many years, I would only remember the angry, frustrating, shameful times that Dad created. As I grew older and matured, I began to remember the dad who was an honorable World War II marine combat veteran; the dad who would often throw a baseball and a football with me; the dad who endearingly made me the child mascot of the football teams he coached (all his players called me "little Shaw"); the dad who bragged about me to anyone who would listen; the dad who was a loyal friend to many; the dad who was a hardworking provider and who held two jobs, and the dad who remained faithful to my mother all the days of their life together. (There was never a time when I feared a broken home. The possibility wasn't even on my radar.) I also know him as the dad who loved me and my brother. That is how I choose to speak of him and honor him now.

I have also come to realize a correlation I did not see before. When I would consider my father (or my mother) in dishonorable terms, things did not go well for me, and I had difficulty securing my purpose. The past several years, despite the constant spiritual warfare that we all experience, I have felt much more fulfillment, peace, and hope about what lies ahead. Spiritual warfare will continue until Jesus' second coming, but why exacerbate the situation by my choices and how I consider my parents? An antagonistic posture toward our parents will negatively affect our purpose. "It is more common today for young people to miss the will of God by forsaking their parents' instruction than to miss His will by putting their parents first" (Rosenbaum 1994, 83).

Young people who have grown up in less than nurturing homes often become deficient parents themselves. Their anger, bitterness, and hurt often flow over into their own parenting style. Unless we deal with our reactions to our parents, regardless of their shortcomings, we will not experience peace and purpose. Thinking the worst of our parents only exacerbates the problem. The chain reaction of upheaval and bad behavior grows, not just in families but in society as a whole. Rosenbaum makes an important observation:

> Reverence for parents is hardly what it was a century—or even a generation—ago. As it has diminished, we have had massive promiscuity, divorce, drug addiction, abortion, and crime. Both our standard of living and our standard of education have declined (Rosenbaum 1994, 26).

So what should we do? How can we rediscover the pathway to our purpose? The way we honor our parents is revealed in the way we honor God. Without such honor, our purpose is hindered. Here are some practical and spiritual essentials to pursue. Be diligent in these pursuits—your purpose and destiny are at stake!

- Ask the Lord Jesus to do a work in your heart as well as your parents' hearts. "Search me, O God, and know my heart; try me and know my anxious thoughts; and see if there be any hurtful way in me, and lead me in the everlasting way" (Ps. 139:23–24). Be aware of your attitude and behavior toward your parent(s); repent of the ones that are sinful and relationship-breaking.

- Forgive your parents for whatever they are truly guilty of.
- Honor and respect your parents and, depending on your stage in life, obey them.
- Reach out to them if they are absent or estranged. To break contact with parents is to dishonor them. Let them know you are willing to dialogue and seek restoration if at all possible.
- Be humble and contrite. "You would not believe, until you have seen it, how the child's obedient spirit opens the heart of the parent" (Rosenbaum 1994, 118).
- Expect the discomfort and broken trust to take some time to heal. But trust will be renewed if both parties are sincere.
- Focus on the present and the future and place the past under the blood of Christ.
- The best way to honor your parents is to honor God with your life.

Parents, here are some ways to help your children. After all, as parents our primary purpose is to love our children, to protect them, to teach and to guide them, and to prepare them for their lives as adults.

- Do not provoke your children to anger (Eph. 6:5). Understand that *provoke* means "to deliberately make someone annoyed or angry" (*Oxford Dictionary* 2002). Most parents are not deliberately out to anger their children. In most cases, children are reacting to parental restrictions.
- Seek forgiveness when you have hurt your children.
- Express your renewed desire to love them and to support them toward their calling. This does not mean that parents should enable irresponsible behavior.
- Value and cherish them.

- If your children are married adults, be a resource to them but not a butinski. Butt out—let them develop their own marriage and parenting styles. You can express concerns, but you cannot dictate to them.
- Pray that they will honor God with their lives. After all, there is no greater honor for you than when your children honor God.

CHAPTER 7

Purpose Busters: Weapons of Satan

> Be of sober spirit, be on the alert. Your adversary, the devil, prowls around like a roaring lion, seeking someone to devour. But resist him, firm in your faith.
> —1 Peter 5:8–9

> The thief comes only to steal, and kill, and destroy.
> —John 10:10

I loved playing electric football. Before video and computer games, there were many games that required more planning and strategy. Electric football was one of them. The game had a flat metal playing field that, once plugged in, would vibrate and could be turned on and off. Each contestant had small plastic figurines that represented football players in different stances. The football was a small cotton swab, which could be carried by some of the figurine players. Once the players were placed on the vibrating playing field, the thin contacts under each of the plastic figurines would cause the figurine to move—sometimes forward, sometimes sideways, sometimes in unpredictable directions.

The object of the game was to provide enough blocking and resistance in front of the ball carrier so that the opposing team could not touch him. Once he was touched, the play was over and the ball was downed at that spot. Typically, each contestant would pile his figurines in clusters, hoping that his cluster would provide the stronger resistance. It would often be several minutes before the figurines would begin to split away from their clusters and either provide an open field for the ball carrier or break through to touch him. The adversary would push against his opponent to prevent forward movement and to force him to move in the opposite direction. The constant adversarial force would determine who won.

We fight a similar spiritual battle. Our adversary, the Devil, is constantly looking to push against us to disrupt God's purpose for our lives. If we try to move forward, he will push back to win. The Bible says, "Submit therefore to God. Resist the devil and he will flee from you" (James 4:7). Through faith, we are to call upon the power of the Holy Spirit to push back and help us reach the divine goal for our lives. We face a constant and often unpredictable battle. Unlike electric football, Satan's strategies are often subtle and hidden, and we do not always see our true enemy.

Satan is always moving against the things of God. He is also seeking to come against us, especially if we are trying to live out our God-given purpose. Satan knows that if men and women are restored to God through Jesus Christ and discover who they really are and where they are going in life, he could be overcome and lose his influence. The Devil sees your potential more clearly than you do. He works feverishly to prevent you from seeing who you are, what you are called to do, and where God has you going. God wants to empower us; Satan wants to render us powerless. The Devil comes only to steal, kill, and destroy. There is no good in him. He never has our best interest in mind.

Satan uses several weapons to achieve his goals and to hinder us. In no particular order, these weapons are:

- doubt
- deception
- discord
- destruction
- discouragement
- distractions

Each of these weapons can be applied to all of our core longings: significance, safety, purpose, understanding, belonging, and love. The Lord is the center of our longings. The Devil is the center of the resistance. Satan is effective in using his weapons to block us and to redirect us away from God. If he is successful, we will think that we have been left to ourselves with no one to depend upon. We will then believe that we have the power to do whatever we want. Independence will become our goal and even our idol. We will seek independence from relationships, from laws, from morals and ethics, and from any absolutes. "Everything is relative" will become our battle cry.

The truth is that no one is independent. We may believe that we are, but each of us is dependent on something or someone. Remember our discussion in chapter 3 regarding idols? Something or someone rules our lives. Our sinful, fallen nature rules our lives with the help of Satan. When we acknowledge that we fall short and that we need a Savior and we ask Jesus Christ to save us and impart to us His nature, we experience dependence upon Him. Dependence upon Jesus is really freedom, because He empowers us. Independence is the perceived power to do what we want. Freedom is the power to do what is right.

Doubt

Our identity and significance are affected by doubt, Satan's weapon. Doubt about God and ourselves causes insecurity, fear, and a lack of confidence. Doubt breeds anxiety. I define *anxiety* as the belief that love, protection, and abundance are in limited supply (Matt 14:31). The word *doubt* in Greek is *distazo* and means "to waver" or "standing uncertainly at two ways" (Weirsbe 2007, 43). We often struggle when we see two ways instead of one—our way, which seems rational but often springs from a self-centered mindset, or Jesus' way, which may defy our own logic and be more than we are able to do.

Peter wavered, unable to hold on to his faith, even though he was walking on the water. He experienced doubt and distraction, which caused him to take his eyes off of Jesus. As a result, Peter sank. Jesus quickly responded. "And immediately Jesus stretched out His hand and took hold of him, and said to him, 'O you of little faith, why do you doubt?'" (Matt. 14:31).

Doubt, therefore, is "double-mindedness," (Phil 4:19). James says:

> But if any of you lacks wisdom, let him ask of God, who gives to all men generously and without reproach, and it will be given unto him. But let him ask in faith without doubting, for the one who doubts is like the surf of the sea driven and tossed by the wind. For let not that man expect that he will receive anything from the Lord, being a double-minded man, unstable in all his ways (James 1:5–8).

Another word for doubt found in the New Testament is *dialogismos*, which means "to argue through reasoning." This is doubt that expects no final answer. A person exhibiting this type of doubt usually is contentious and is looking for an argument. The word is found in 1 Timothy 2:8: "Therefore I want the men in every place to pray, lifting up holy hands, without wrath and dissention." Arguing brings discord, another weapon of Satan. This kind of doubt leaves the person suspended in uncertainty, unable to reach a conviction.

This type of doubt reigns in academia. Scholars and professors perpetuate doubts and raise countless questions. We are told to question authority, question institutions, question absolutes. But are we ever given answers? No! Scholars who claim they have the answers are labeled as narrow-minded and backward. The charge is most often leveled at Christians. In past centuries, wise men and women were those who had more answers than questions. Today, men and women are considered wise if they have more questions than answers. The apostle Paul, a scholarly man, described such people well: "always learning and never able to come to the knowledge of the truth" (2 Tim. 3:7).

Without conviction, purpose in life is hard to come by. Where there is doubt, we are tossed about by whatever wind comes our way. James 1:6 says, "But let him ask in faith without any doubting, for the one who doubts is like the surf of the sea driven and tossed by the wind." Instead of questioning authority and rebelling, we need to honor authority.

Luke 12:29 uses another word for doubt: "And do not seek what you shall eat, and what you shall drink, and do not keep worrying." The Greek word is *meteorizo* from which we get the word *meteor*. The word connotes a condition of uncertainty, as if "suspended in the air." That is a great way to describe worry—as if our thoughts and emotions are suspended in the air. The serpent generated uncertainty and worry in Eve and Adam. He told them that the fruit was forbidden not because God desired their protection and well-being, but because God did not want them to be like Him. They worried that God was holding out on them and decided that they needed to take for themselves. Such doubt leads to self-centered decisions.

If doubt rules our lives, we fear rejection. "Soon we become utterly confused as to who we really are and can be controlled, almost completely, by external circumstances" (Joyner 1993, 36). We wonder if we are loved and if there is anywhere we belong. We doubt that anyone understands us and what we are experiencing. We doubt we are secure in relationships and fear we may never be. Finally, if doubt exists, we may question not only what our purpose may be but whether we even have a purpose.

Deception

Satan deceives us into believing that we have sinned too much to be redeemed by God. We have been deceived that there is no God. We are deceived to believe we have no sin. "If we say that we have no sin, we are deceiving ourselves, and the truth is not in us" (1 John 1:8). We can be deceived that the world, fame, and riches lead to our identity and significance. "Deception is not just misunderstanding a doctrine; it is not being in His will" (Joyner 1993, 53). Not being in the will of God alters our purpose and leads to frustration, misery, and evil.

The Hebrew word *nasha* means "to lead astray." Jeremiah 49:16 says, "The arrogance of your heart has deceived you." People are often deceived in relationships and discover that someone is not as advertised. This often happens with a controlling and abusive person. The person may appear strong and safe but will turn out to be abusive and oppressive.

Some of the most powerful deceptions involve what is right and wrong. This is why God's law must have a place once again in our lives. Jesus Christ, who fulfilled the law, provides purpose, identity, understanding, love, safety, and a sense of belonging, and meets our longings in life.

In recent history Sigmund Freud was one of the most powerful influences on how humans understand right and wrong. When we do something right, we know it and it feels good. This is called our conscience. It is the part of our spirit that somehow knows we are in the image of Him who truly knows right and wrong. Freud took a different approach, and many people and cultures still buy into it. "Instead of teaching that the relief from guilt and resulting depression was to be found in doing what is right, he began to attack what he considered unrealistic morals and standards" (Joyner 1993, 37).

Freud's answer was to eliminate life-giving standards. This philosophy has led people to question authority, parents, God, and morals. Satan has gradually and deceptively introduced this philosophy into our culture, and it has now become the standard. After all, this philosophy says, if there are no standards of right and wrong, then we have no reason to feel guilt and shame. Everything is relative.

While it is true that none of us can live up to the law of God on our own, the answer is not to remove the standards, thus providing a perception of freedom. Instead we must admit that we cannot live by such standards and that we need a Savior who can cleanse us and grant us power—His power—to live according to His ways. Joyner observes:

> The more we seek to ignore the Law, the more depressed and schizophrenic we will become. The philosophy of 'removing the ancient boundaries' is in some form permeating every society of the world. The 'deep darkness' that was prophesied to come over the world is being released (Isa. 60:2) (Joyner 1993, 39).

Freud was advocating independence, not freedom. Independence is the belief that we can do whatever we want with no constraints. Freedom is the power to do what is right. Freedom helps us achieve our purpose. Independence leads us into lawlessness, chaos, deception, and confusion. Our purpose is not tied to the elimination of constraints. Our purpose is tied to experiencing the freedom that empowers us.

The truth is we all live with constraints. Even people who are liberal and "progressive" in their thinking would be disingenuous if they did not acknowledge that constraints help stabilize a society. Without constraints there would be no purpose, which would create anarchy.

If we drove outside the highway lines, we would have car wrecks on a regular basis. Highways have speed limits, or constraints. Of course, we like to go beyond such constraints, and if caught by the highway patrol, we have to pay a hefty fine and perhaps lose our privilege to drive for a while. We never consider that when we arrive at the store, we automatically park within the white lines of a parking space—usually without complaint. The white lines represent constraints.

We also face financial constraints (we can't overdraw our bank accounts without penalties); travel constraints (carry-on luggage must be within a certain size); relationship constraints (almost all cultures honor the one wife/one husband arrangement, with penalties for affairs); and legal constraints (we can't walk into someone's house and steal a television, jewelry, and a laptop without going to jail if caught). These are just a few of the countless constraints, many of which we simply accept without a thought as a part of our lifestyle. Few people would disagree that these constraints are beneficial.

The laws of every country are designed to provide constraints to keep order and safety but also to provide freedom to live our purpose.

111

A human being is not "truly free to live in this world without the restrictions that God has placed upon him. The very constraints which confine man [also] set him free to be what he was created to be" (Joyner 1993, 39). Our purpose is at stake. We need to return to the standards of God through Jesus.

Deception can affect each of our core longings. For example, we may be deceived into believing that someone understands us when the person is manipulative or may be ignoring us. We may be deceived into thinking that we understand a situation but instead may see the whole thing blow up in our faces.

We may be deceived that we have been accepted into a group and feel a sense of belonging, only to learn that we were accepted because of what someone wanted from us. True acceptance and sense of belonging occur when we are in a group, family, church, or club because we are sincerely cherished as individuals. We may be deceived into placing significance upon a title or an achievement, only to realize that these things are short-lived.

We may be deceived that we are loved when all the other person wanted was sex. We may also be deceived that we love someone else when we may only be dependent, perhaps using this person to get us out of a bad situation.

We may be deceived regarding our purpose, going along with someone else's idea about what we should do and where we should go. Such deception can be devastating, leading to a frustrating endeavor and a waste of precious time, money, and energy. God is our ultimate guide toward our purpose, and He may use parents, leaders, and significant trusted people in our lives to encourage and instruct us. The Lord, however, calls us first to Himself and then to what He has in store for us.

Discord

Satan will use conflict and discord to thwart us. He attacks through offenses. The way we respond to offenses will determine our future. When discord occurs, emotions may range from discomfort to outright hatred, causing a desire for revenge. Our destiny, safety, and sense of love and belonging can be altered as a result. The Devil will use discord to prevent, or at least detour, our purpose and to render us hurt and frustrated. As a result, we may feel trapped and immobilized emotionally and mentally. The apostle James wrote, "But if you have bitter jealousy [envy] and selfish ambition in your heart, do not be arrogant and so lie against the truth … For where jealousy [envy] and selfish ambition exist, there is disorder and every evil thing" (James 3:14, 16).

Discord can have the effect of stereotyping all situations, all men, all churches, or all leaders, leading us to believe that nothing can be different from what we know and have experienced. "All men will hurt me." "All churches are alike." "She does this all the time." "He will never change." "I can never forgive what he/she did to me." These are some of many things that we say when we hold on to offenses. Clinging to such beliefs gets in the way of fulfilling our purpose. "All" and "never" rarely apply to anything in life. When I meet with couples, I often hear "He never does this or that" or "She always does this or that." The first thing I challenge is the "all" or "never" claim.

Discord is a weapon that often shows up in marriages. When husband and wife are in conflict, the emotional, mental, and sometimes physical impact can be huge. We become angry, resentful, hurt, and vindictive. As a result, we are easily discouraged and distracted. Our lives become engrossed in the conflict and our purpose becomes clouded. Because of the relational and financial impact, we may have to give up the pursuit of our purpose, or at least place it on hold, if divorce happens.

When marital discord occurs, it is important to seek counseling early to prevent growing resentment. Your purpose together, as well as personally, may be at stake. You do not want the Devil to derail your calling in life.

Discord is a weapon that Satan uses in families. If he can orchestrate discord in families, many other relationships will be affected. If children of any age have conflicts with their parents, the effect is often deep and wide. Sometimes the discord occurs because of rebellion in the young person. Sometimes discord occurs because of abuse by the parent. If discord is allowed to linger and fester, the child or the adult child is usually affected more than the parent. The antidotes to discord are honesty, forgiveness, and restoration. As long as discord remains, our purpose in life is hindered. We cannot feel free to be all we can be, because of discord in the most important relationships we will ever have. I have found that if Satan cannot dissolve a marriage, he goes after family relationships.

Discord can occur in the church and in the workplace. Politics and favoritism can often lead to conflict. Discord may often prevent a promotion, job movement, and pursuit of one's true purpose. I have been overlooked and falsely accused of certain things. As I noted in chapter 1, I had to seek God many times. I needed Him to encourage me that my purpose was in His control, that He had my life in His hands, and that He was aware of the discord and injustice that took place. He is a God who sees. He is a God who cares. He is a God whose purposes cannot be thwarted. The Lord will show you how to conduct yourself and tell if you should wait on Him or move on to pursue your purpose.

Discord often arises when family members are about to receive an inheritance from a deceased relative. Survivors may become greedy for what they believe is coming to them. Such discord can be especially contentious and even life-altering. It surely does not need to be. The same can be said for our spiritual inheritance. Church folk can often sow discord because of envy over someone else's role, favor, and blessings. The good news is that in the kingdom of God, there is no limit to our inheritance or to our impact. There will always be room for everyone to receive God's love, grace, and blessings. We do not have to experience discord as long we take our eyes off of others. God has His own purpose for each of us. We will not be left out as long as we keep our hopes and desires focused upon Him.

What makes this weapon so diabolical is that discord often occurs between family and friends. Consider one of David's psalms:

> For it is not an enemy that reproaches me, then I could bear it; nor is it one who hates me who has exalted himself against me, then I could hide myself from him. But it is you, a man my equal, my companion and my familiar friend. We who had sweet fellowship together, walked in the house of God in throng (Ps. 55:12–14).

Discord can be especially immobilizing when it occurs between individuals or groups that had lived or worked together well in the past. The Devil especially tries to render such individuals and groups ineffective when their successes have challenged his kingdom of darkness. Individuals and groups then may see their purpose hindered and delayed. Unfortunately, Satan has been good at subtly infusing discord into situations. We must remember that we do not "struggle against flesh and blood, but against the rulers, against the powers, against the world forces of this darkness, against the spiritual forces of wickedness in the heavenly places" (Eph. 6:12).

Offended people, as well as offenders, will bear much fruit. Unfortunately, it is the wrong kind of fruit. Galatians 5:19–21 says, "Now the deeds of the flesh are evident, which are: sexual immorality, impurity, sensuality, idolatry, sorcery, *enmities, strife, jealousy, outbursts of anger, disputes, dissensions, factions,* envying, drunkenness, carousing, and things like these" (emphasis mine). Discord appears in people who are hurtful, fickle, disagreeable, arrogant, and oppositional. The resulting experiences are strife, division, defamation, slander, blame, censure, and sarcasm. All have a strong effect on us related to our core longings. This spirit of discord never allows a person's life to continue in peace. Instead, discord will disturb peace. Using this weapon, Satan breaks down family relationships and will attempt to destroy all things that are good.

We need to pray every day and bind up all lies from the attacking spirit that produces discord. God is bigger than our offenses. Forgiveness and our resolve not to "take into account a wrong suffered" (1 Cor. 13:5) will prevent a seed of bitterness from being planted. One of the Devil's lies is that we are getting back at those who hurt us by withholding forgiveness or by holding on to grudges. In fact, we are hurting ourselves when we hold on to offenses. Holding on to that anger prevents us from being able to forgive the perpetrator.

Research has shown that the stress that accompanies suppressed anger resulting from unforgiveness can lead to mental and physical problems. Some studies have even suggested that anger directly increases a person's risk for cardiovascular disease (GoodTherapy. org, 2012). Barry points out,

> Harboring these negative emotions, this anger and hatred, creates a state of chronic anxiety. Chronic anxiety very predictably produces excess adrenaline and cortisol, which

deplete the production of natural killer cells which is your
body's foot soldier in the fight against cancer (Barry 2011).

Our ability to hear from God and fulfill purpose is hampered. The lying spirit must be bound so that truth will prevail in all situations. The perverse spirit must be bound so there will be no twisting of words or actions, opening the way for offenses. Discord must be bound so that this spirit doesn't hinder the pursuit of our purpose. The spirit of discord often is accompanied by a spirit of discouragement, a spirit of doubt, and/or a spirit of destruction.

Destruction

Destruction is often related to discord. The Hebrew word *abad*, usually rendered as "destroy," often refers to violent action causing physical death (Num. 16:33; Ps. 2:12). But less intense meanings may be denoted. Exodus 10:7 describes economic ruin, as does Matthew 9:17, using the Greek word *apollumi*. In the New Testament, the common Greek word for destroy is *katargeo*, which can mean "render powerless" or "ineffective" (Heb. 2:14).

If discord festers long enough, the desire to destroy emerges. Discord can have a strong effect on our core longings. This is especially true of our sense of belonging and of our purpose. If we allow discord, offense, and hurt to linger, resentment and bitterness develop. Once bitterness develops, the next step is vengeance. The desire for revenge is a distraction and often becomes our purpose. Vengeance leads to destruction.

Vengeance is never satisfied. When have we had enough vengeance? Do we not desire to continue "paying back" others for their offenses, continuing the destruction of relationships? Yes, payback feels good. However, it feels better when we release and forgive and are freed. Otherwise, a spirit of vindictiveness often develops. Vindictiveness is an ongoing desire for vengeance.

It often starts in the family. "God created the family. Therefore, the devil is always at work to destroy it. The alienation of husband and wife is what he desires most. Next to that he seeks to estrange children from their parents" (Rosenbaum 1994, 106). Jesus said, "The thief only comes to steal, and kill, and destroy" (John 10:10). A thief will break into a house or a store only if he believes that there is good stuff inside. The family, as God designed it, is the foundation of society. In fact, after each day of His creation, God said it was "good," and after He created man and woman on the sixth day, He said it was "very good" (Gen. 1:31).

The man and woman as husband and wife are the foundation of what is very good in God's design for the world. The redefining of what constitutes a family is a diabolical scheme that will have nothing but bad consequences. Leviticus 18 lists the Canaanites' abominations as incest, homosexuality, adultery, child sacrifice, and bestiality. Because of this immorality, the land vomited them out. No society can tolerate such destruction of family life for long.

In Revelation 9:1, 11, the king of the bottomless pit is called Abaddon, which means "destruction." It is a characteristic and a name given to Satan himself. It is not by chance that one of the Devil's names in Scripture means destruction. Again, John 10:10 says, "The thief comes only to steal, and kill, and destroy." A broken relationship between husband and wife can bring destruction to the family through divorce, vindictiveness between the parties, rebellious children, and financial difficulties, just to name few consequences. Love is destroyed. All involved lose a sense of belonging and of safety. Their sense of significance or identity is altered. They are left feeling alone and believe that no one understands them.

Broken relationships between families can bring destruction when feuds lead to the loss of life and property. Consider the Mafia— basically families warring over the exploitation of sinful behaviors. They destroy one another after quarrels lead to vengeance. The news is replete with reports of violent domestic disputes that often result in the destruction of innocent people. Broken relationships between nations can bring destruction through violent uprisings and wars. All of this has a devastating effect upon a person's purpose, a family's purpose, and even a nation's purpose.

Picking up the pieces of what destruction leaves behind can take time, often resulting in a hindered purpose. Floods, tornadoes, and other disasters can destroy homes, businesses, and lives. As a result, our purpose can seemingly be destroyed. It is imperative that we work to rebuild what was destroyed and bring into existence something new. God is still in the redeeming business! There are times, however, when God will work through destruction. Something may have to be destroyed to bring forth God's purpose. Such occasions are among the most difficult to deal with in life. Faced with these experiences, we need to remember that God works "all things together for good" (Rom. 8:28).

Discouragement

Satan is very good at orchestrating events that prevent us from fulfilling our desires. Paul records in 1 Thessalonians 2:18 his hope to visit the believers to whom he was writing, "and yet Satan thwarted us." Nevertheless he expressed hope, and even though he was not able to preach the gospel in Thessalonica and encourage the believers, he was able to send Timothy to do so. Although Paul was disappointed, his purpose was still achieved by sending someone he knew could do what he would have done (1 Thess. 3:1–5). When Timothy returned to Paul, the report he gave about his trip "comforted" Paul and dispelled his disappointment (1 Thess. 3:6–8).

The diabolical aspect of disappointment is that it can lead to discouragement, which then can lead to depression. Disappointment occurs in a moment and over one situation. Discouragement takes hold when disappointments pile up, making us reluctant to dream and to try again for fear of experiencing the same result. Depression kicks in when we believe that no matter what we do, things will not change and we will always suffer disappointment and hurt. We lose heart and become stuck. Depression is an emotional response to any loss. When we try and fail or when someone hurts us, we may feel like our lives have been ruined. As a result, regaining our drive to find and fulfill our purpose becomes more difficult. Depression can affect not only our purpose but our relationships. Our purpose is dead in the water when depression sets in, and the Devil has won. Depression leaves us immobilized and ineffective.

We will all experience disappointments throughout life. They will happen as long as we live in this broken world. How we recover from disappointments is critical. We do not have to allow disappointments to sink into discouragement and then into depression. Disappointments do not have to be devastating. Once again living life according to God's blueprint will often be the medicine we need. We do not have to add any more dramatics to the disappointments we experience. Disappointments are not the last word about anything. God has a purpose for our lives, and He will be sure to see it through.

Distractions

Distractions come in countless forms and can cause us to be derailed, detoured, and preoccupied. They are often an attack by the Enemy. When we feel pressures over money, health, relationships, marriage, or children, the Devil will use these problems to torment us with the spirit of distraction. Paul dealt with this in Philippi.

> Once when we were going to the place of prayer, we were met by a slave girl who had a spirit by which she predicted the future. She earned a great deal of money for her owners by fortune-telling. This girl followed Paul and the rest of us, shouting, "These men are servants of the Most High God, who are telling you the way to be saved." She kept this up for many days. Finally Paul became so troubled that he turned around and said to the spirit, "In the name of Jesus Christ I command you to come out of her!" At that moment the spirit left her. (Acts 16:16–18)

Even though she was declaring a truth that Paul and his companions were servants of God, the girl was a distraction. She was causing others to divert their gaze to her, lessening the effectiveness of the preaching of the gospel. Paul dealt directly with the distraction. Many who face this spirit do not. We often are so busy, even doing church work, that we miss true relationship with Jesus and the peace in our lives that comes as a result. If you are under stress and are in ministry, you must take authority over this. Stress will immobilize you or worse, cause you to react by manifesting in the spirit of distraction. The best response to the spirit of distraction is intentional calm and direct confrontation of the tormentor.

The spirit of distraction tells us that we have to be full of activity to be accepted by God. The lie is that the more we do, the more God accepts us. Sooner or later we experience burnout, or "compassion fatigue," as those in counseling call it. When that occurs, we become worn-out, disappointed, and frustrated. Such distractions keep us from enjoying the Sabbath, which brings the inner rest and peace that we experience when we know we are in God's presence and enjoy a secure relationship with Him.

We are distracted by television, cell phones, the Internet, entertainment, games, the accumulation of "stuff," and whatever we deem urgent. This young generation is especially distracted by computer games, tweeting, blogging, and pornography. With kids ages eight to eighteen spending on average 44.5 hours per week in front of screens, parents are increasingly concerned that this time is robbing them of real-world experiences. Nearly 23 percent of youngsters report that they feel "addicted to video games" (31 percent of males, 13 percent of females). These are the results of a 2007 study of 1,178 US children and teens (ages eight to eighteen) conducted by Harris Interactive that documents pathological video game use. Dr. Douglas Gentile, a leading researcher and director of the Media Research Lab at Iowa State University, reports, "Almost one out of every ten youth gamers shows enough symptoms of damage to their school, family, and psychological functioning to merit serious concern" (Gentile 2003).

Our dependence on technology and entertainment manifests the spirit of distraction. The apostle John makes a poignant declaration:

> For all that is in the world, the lust of the flesh and the lust of the eyes and boastful pride of life, is not from the Father, but from the world. And the world is passing away, and also its lusts; but the one who does the will of God abides forever (1 John 2:16–17).

Coveting and distractions are often related. We are distracted by the desire to accumulate stuff. The stuff we often desire is what we see others have. Worldly trinkets, big possessions, an often unrealistic body type, and power and influence are some of the many things we lust for. Lust is motivated by getting; love is motivated by giving. Acts 20:35 says, "In everything I showed you that by working hard in this manner you must help the weak and remember the words of the Lord Jesus, that He Himself said, 'It is more blessed to give that to receive.'"

Jesus said, "Beware and be on your guard against every form of greed; for not even when one has an abundance does his life consist of his possessions" (Luke 12:15). Do we have stuff, or does stuff have us? How was our abundance obtained, and what are we purposing to do with all that we have? Do we plan to give to be a blessing to others, or will we walk in the "boastful pride of life"? When we are distracted, our purpose is often altered to be about getting. True purpose is about giving. That is God's heart. That is His desire for us as well.

While all of these weapons of Satan affect each of our core longings, each weapon has an effect on one longing in particular. As I consider the scriptural accounts of people, all the experiences I have had in life, as well as all of the people I have known in and out of counseling and ministry, I would list each weapon of Satan with its most direct effect as follows:

Doubt has perhaps the greatest effect on: **Significance**
Deception has perhaps the greatest effect on: **Understanding**
Destruction has perhaps the greatest effect on: **Safety**
Discord has perhaps the greatest effect on: **Love**
Discouragement has perhaps the greatest effect on: **Belonging**
Distractions have perhaps the greatest effect on: **Purpose**

Satan will often pile on and use multiple weapons. For example, when discord occurs, those involved in the conflict often feel discouraged. Once they feel discouraged, doubt about their purpose may be close behind. The area directly related to our purpose often becomes a target of the Devil. For example, if you are called to be a social worker or a counselor, the Devil may undermine your relationships, especially in your family. Such a frontal attack can raise doubts about your credibility. If you are a business owner and serve the Lord and others with excellence, the Devil may attack your cash flow, your employees, or your equipment.

Distraction, discouragement, and doubt can happen at once and feel overwhelming. The Devil's intent is to hinder your effectiveness. Satan's desire is to immobilize us and cause us to be ineffective. He will not play fair. The good news is that we can overcome such tactics by the truth and the power of God through Christ, for "greater is He who is you than he who is in the world" (1 John 4:4).

If we can put fears, envy, insecurity, doubt, disappointments, discord, distractions, deceptions, destruction, and self-centeredness aside, purpose will emerge as a result. Much of our purpose is to fight against the wiles of the Devil so that we can remain steadfast in Christ.

- No need to perform—Christ did it.
- No need to seek approval—Christ gives it.
- No need to punish—Christ took it.
- No need to feel hopeless—Christ can do it.

Finally, consider what the apostle Peter wrote,

> Humble yourself, therefore, under the mighty hand of God, that He may exalt you at the proper time, casting all your anxiety upon Him, because He cares for you. Be of sober spirit, be on the alert. Your adversary, the devil, prowls about like a roaring lion, seeking someone to devour. But resist him, firm in your faith, knowing that the same experiences of suffering are being accomplished by your brethren who are in the world. And after you have suffered for a little while, the God of all grace, who called you to His eternal glory in Christ, will Himself perfect, confirm, strengthen and establish you. (1 Peter 5:6–10)

CHAPTER 8

Knowing Our Passions, Temperaments, and Gifts

But seek first His kingdom and His righteousness; and all these things shall be added to you.

—Matt. 6:33

Delight yourself in the Lord and He will give you the desires of your heart.

—Ps. 37:4

Be transformed by the renewing of your mind, that you may prove what the will of God is, that which is good, and acceptable, and perfect.

—Rom. 12:2

Owning a home is a challenge and a blessing at the same time. It can be exciting and stressful. Once the papers are signed at closing (and today there are more than an hour's worth of papers to review and sign), moving in and making your house your home can be rewarding and fulfilling. I know it is for me. My wife especially enjoys putting her touch on the home, which I have come to appreciate.

However, my body reacts badly to certain aspects of home-ownership. I am not handy with tools. Whenever something needs repair, my hearts sinks and I sometimes feel a gut wrench. I have been forced to do maintenance in the past and did well (most of the time) in completing these tasks. After all, it is often more practical to just do it yourself than to spend the money on repairs. Such is the life of a homeowner. But I still dislike the tasks.

I do enjoy yard work and room painting—I even enjoy painting the molding and the trim. But when it comes to repairs, I will seek out those who enjoy the work and can do a better job than I can. Interestingly enough, people who can do plumbing, electrical work, construction, and roof repairs have often told me that they hate painting. When I tell them I will be painting their finished work, they have the same reaction to painting that I have about carpentry and plumbing.

And when home improvement and repair people learn that I am a minister and a Christian counselor, they often recoil and ask how I can listen to people tell me their problems all day. Their reaction to what I do is like mine when it comes to home improvements—they would rather work with tools than with people. I would rather work with people than with tools. This illustrates the differences between individuals based upon temperament, gifts, passions, and purpose.

Temperament is the combination of inborn traits that subconsciously affect people's behavior (LaHaye 1991, 12). Temperaments are passed on by genes and can be as unpredictable as eye color, hair, and body size. Even though these traits are genetically determined, they can be changed. According to Dr. Anita Remig, a professor and researcher at the University of New Hampshire, genes are not the "powerful dictators" they were originally thought to be. They are more like "blueprints" and "potentials" (Remig 2010). The psychosocial environment (family, culture, and social environment) is critical, even as it relates to the gene effect.

Character is the "real you" (LaHaye 1991, 12). It is the result of natural temperament affected by childhood upbringing, education, and basic attitudes, belief system, and motivation. The Bible calls it the "hidden person of the heart" (1 Peter 3:4). The "old nature" or the sinful nature of man is our character.

It is imperative, therefore, for us to surrender to and accept Jesus Christ so that a new nature or character can develop. He provides a new nature when we acknowledge that we are sinners in need of a savior and ask Him to save us and to rule and guide our lives. Our character, or what I call our "substance," is altered as we allow Christ to transform us to be more like Him. That is our primary purpose—to reflect Jesus in our lives—and only the Holy Spirit can make the changes within us to achieve our purpose. Many people present themselves in a certain way, and it is substance that maintains the consistency of what they show to others. Otherwise, it is all a façade.

Our personalities are simply outward expressions of who we are, which may or may not be the same as our character, depending on how genuine we are (LaHaye 1991, 12). The Bible says, "For God sees not as man sees, for man looks at the outward appearance, but the Lord looks at the heart" (1 Sam. 16:7). What we show others is not necessarily what resides in our hearts.

Even if men are not able to discern the dichotomy within an individual, Jesus surely can. In Matthew 15:8 Jesus says, "This people honors Me with their lips, but their heart is far from me." He was separating the personality, what one shows outwardly, from the character, what exists in the heart. The more we allow God's Holy Spirit to affect our temperament and to mold our character, the more we will show forth a personality that is God-centered and lines up with our changing spirit.

For many centuries, we have operated with the theory that there are four basic temperaments in human beings. Hippocrates (460–370 BC), a Greek physician and philosopher, was the first to present the theory of four temperaments. Later, Galen (AD 129–216), a Greek-speaking Roman physician and philosopher, coined the terms for the four temperaments that we know today. Hippocrates and Galen erroneously thought that these temperaments were the result of the four liquids that are predominant in the human body: blood (sanguine), choler (yellow bile), melancholy (black bile), and phlegm (LaHaye 1991, 16). "The idea that temperament is determined by body liquid has long been discarded, but strangely enough, the four-fold classification of temperaments is still widely used" (LaHaye 1991, 16). Our temperaments are a part of who we are and contribute to our personalities. The four temperaments are sanguine, choleric, melancholy, and phlegmatic.

The temperaments can be briefly described as follows:

- Sanguine are people-oriented, outgoing types who excel in public relations, people-helping, or anything that requires an outgoing approach and charisma. They have enthusiasm and are action-oriented. They can also be emotional, restless, forgetful, and undisciplined and may often talk about themselves.
- Cholerics are natural leaders who are goal-oriented or project-oriented and who like to manage people. They are self-disciplined, good leaders, and show strong determination. They can be tenacious, hardworking, but also impetuous, grudge-holding, and unrepentant and may break the law to meet their needs.

- Melancholics are creative, analytical people with strong perfectionistic tendencies who often have aesthetic traits. They are sensitive, discerning, reflective, faithful in relationships, have a high standard of excellence, and seek to better their fellow human beings. They can also be vain, pessimistic, overly critical, and easily depressed and may harbor resentment.

- Phlegmatics are cool, detailed individuals who tend to limit themselves. They can do statistical, microscopic work that would drive others berserk. They are easygoing, practical, and dependable, work well under pressure, and are good listeners. They can also be slow or lazy, sarcastic, selfish, unteachable, and indecisive. (LaHaye 1994, 353–354)

These four temperaments can be clustered by two, providing a framework for noticing individual tendencies. Up to twelve combinations are possible and help form a person's temperament.

These temperaments, as well as personality tests such as the often-used Myers-Briggs Type Indicator (MBTI), can provide a basic framework to help identify the characteristics of individuals. Katherine Briggs and Isabel Myers pinpointed personality types through their study of the works of Carl Jung. Briggs and Myers began to measure personality types in the early 1940s to help people choose suitable work and to promote the positive use of differences among people.

The MBTI, first published for general use in 1962 by the Educational Testing Service, measures four basic "dichotomies," and several combinations based upon one's personality. The essence of the theory is that much seemingly random variation in behavior is actually quite orderly and consistent. Such patterns can be due to the ways an individual's personality affects thoughts and behavior.

The four dichotomies are described below.

- Extraversion (E)   vs.   (I) Introversion
- Sensing (S)   vs.   (N) Intuition
- Thinking (T)   vs.   (F) Feeling
- Judging (J)   vs.   (P) Perception

E/I

The first dichotomy reflects what generally energizes a person. Extraverted types learn best by talking and interacting with others. By interacting with the physical world, extraverts can process and make sense of new information. Introverted types prefer quiet reflection and privacy. Introverts process information as they explore ideas internally, often in solitude.

S/N

The second dichotomy reflects what a person focuses attention on. Sensing types enjoy a learning environment in which the material is presented in a detailed and sequential manner. Sensing types often attend to what is occurring in the present and can move to the abstract after they have established a concrete experience. Intuitive types prefer a learning atmosphere that emphasizes meaning and associations. They value insight over careful observation, and pattern recognition comes naturally to them.

T/F

The third dichotomy reflects a person's decision preferences. Thinking types desire objective truth and logical principles and are natural at deductive reasoning. Feeling types emphasize issues and causes that can be personalized, and they consider other people's motives.

J/P

The fourth dichotomy reflects how a person regards complexity. Judging types will thrive when information is structured, and they will be motivated to complete assignments to gain closure. Perceiving types will flourish in a flexible learning environment where they are stimulated by new and exciting ideas.

No one is a single temperament or personality type. We all are a mixture. However, one type is usually predominant. All types have their strengths and weaknesses. Knowing about personality types helps us to understand and appreciate differences between people, to learn our own preferences, and to help identify the jobs and vocations for which our temperament may suit us. Since all types are equal, there is no best type. It is important to note that the MBTI sorts for preferences and does not measure traits, ability, or character. To be measured by the MBTI, a person can seek out a licensed psychologist or counselor who is certified to administer the assessment or can go online and take a version of the MBTI there. Many corporations use the MBTI in their company planning and personnel development.

Based upon these types and the mixtures of subtypes, a person can often discover the sort of people he or she may be drawn to, what jobs he or she may like, and what hobbies he or she may enjoy. Knowing one's personality type can help with planning at every stage, from choices of subjects and majors in school, to choosing a first career, to advancing in an organization, to changing careers later in life.

Here is a list of potential jobs and vocations related to primary temperament. Keep in mind that these tendencies are not etched in stone. God can adjust tendencies according His purposes and our benefit.

- **Choleric**: leadership positions, supervisors, business owners, construction workers, developers, entrepreneurs, preachers, military leaders. These people are self-motivated and motivate others and enjoy highly productive work. They have a "get it done" mindset, and they may be hard to please, self-absorbed, and not good at giving compliments and encouragement.

- **Melancholic**: composers, artists, musicians, inventors, philosophers, architects, theologians, educators, engineers, scientists, horticulturalists, mechanics, physicians, nurses, and any vocation that requires perfection, self-sacrifice, and creativity propelled by a heart driven to help others.

- **Phlegmatic**: elementary school teachers, librarians, counselors, school administrators, college department heads, civil engineers, statisticians, foremen, diplomats, and supervisors who work well with people because they are unabrasive, bring order out of chaos, and are extremely dependable. This category also includes jobs that appear to have security built in to them like civil service positions, the military, and local government. These people are not usually risk takers.

- **Sanguine**: sales people, actors and actresses, entertainers, evangelists, auctioneers, masters of ceremonies, politicians, some nurses and hospital workers. These people have a glow to them and like to serve other people and make them happy. They possess natural charisma and a positive attitude. They are good leaders but tend to be a bit shallow; they are better leaders when blended with another temperament.

Our temperament and personality may correlate to the spiritual gifts listed in Scripture and to the gifts we have been given by God. The spiritual gifts are found in Romans 12:3–9, 1 Corinthians 12:7–31, and Ephesians 4:11–13. These God-given gifts are to be used for the common good:

- **Administration**: the ability to understand what makes an organization function and to plan and execute procedures that accomplish the organization's goals.
- **Apostleship**: the ability to start and oversee the development of new churches or ministries.
- **Craftsmanship**: the ability to creatively design and/or construct items to be used for the benefit of others.
- **Creative Communication**: the ability to communicate God's truth through a variety of art forms.
- **Discernment**: the ability to distinguish between truth and error, good and evil, right and wrong, and to discern the spirits.
- **Encouragement**: the ability to present truth so as to strengthen, comfort, or urge to action those who are discouraged and wavering in their faith.
- **Evangelism**: the ability to effectively communicate the gospel to unbelievers so they respond in faith and move toward discipleship.
- **Faith**: the special ability to act on God's promises with confidence and unwavering belief in His ability to fulfill those promises.

- **Giving**: the ability to contribute money, time, and resources with cheerfulness and liberality, especially in doing the work of the Lord.
- **Healing**: the ability to be God's means for restoring people to health and wholeness.
- **Help**: the ability to attach spiritual value to the accomplishment of practical and necessary tasks that meet the needs of others.
- **Hospitality**: the ability to care for people by providing fellowship, food, and shelter.
- **Intercession**: the ability to consistently pray on behalf of and for others, thus seeing frequent and specific results.
- **Interpretation**: the ability to make known to the body of Christ the message of one who has spoken in tongues.
- **Leadership**: the ability to show vision and to motivate and direct people to harmoniously accomplish a common goal.
- **Mercy**: the ability to cheerfully and practically help those who are suffering and in need.
- **Miracles**: the ability to authenticate the ministry and message of God through signs, wonders, and supernatural interventions that glorify Him.
- **Prophecy**: the ability to reveal truth and proclaim it in a timely and relevant manner for understanding, correction, repentance, or edification.
- **Shepherding**: the ability to gather, nurture, and guide people toward ongoing growth, especially as it relates to spiritual maturity and becoming like Christ.
- **Teaching**: the ability to understand, organize, clearly explain, and apply information, concepts, and truth to others; a good teacher helps others gain knowledge and understanding.

- **Tongues:** the ability to speak, worship, or pray in a language unknown to the speaker.
- **Wisdom:** the ability to practically apply spiritual knowledge and truth effectively to meet a need in a specific situation (Bugbee 1995, 61).

Our temperament may allow for the emergence of spiritual gifts that are manifested differently from person to person. Because we are uniquely created, specific gifts will exist in us. Gifts are given by God to be used for the purpose of benfitting others. The apostle Peter says,

> As each one has received a special gift, employ it in serving one another, as good stewards of the manifold grace of God. Whoever speaks, let him speak, as it were, the utterances of God; whoever serves, let him do so as by the strength which God supplies; so that in all things God may be glorified through Jesus Christ, to whom belongs the glory and dominion forever and ever. Amen (1 Peter 4:10–11).

Everyone has been given gifts by God. No one is without something to offer, something to grow into, or something at which he or she can be successful. We all have a purpose. We must not let our gift or purpose be snuffed out. Paul encourages us, saying, "Do not neglect the spiritual gift within you" (1 Tim. 4:14).

The temperament indicator and the MBTI are simple guides and are not valid indicators of job performance, nor can they determine a person's character or overall makeup. But if people are operating within their passion and purpose, they will often work with enthusiasm, motivation, and grace. The temperament guide and the MBTI can be fun and interesting to use for a snapshot of how we are wired, but God is still the only valid resource to help us determine who we are and where we are going.

I have an aversion to labels of any kind, especially since they obscure the truth that we are created in the image of God. So I encourage everyone to see characteristics simply as tools to help us understand who we are and to recognize our tendencies. They are an explanation, but they are not determinants! God determines our inner man and inner woman. Our tendencies can be changed as we surrender to Christ. He transforms the inner person from a nature of sin and rebellion into someone more like Himself. He is our Creator, and as such, knows our tendencies, our gifts, our strengths and weaknesses, and our destiny. To hear from the Lord is essential in determining our purpose.

LaHaye provides seven helpful steps to finding your purpose. First, establish your primary purpose in life, which is the same for all of us. Matthew 6:33 says, "But seek first His kingdom and His righteousness, and all these things shall be added to you." We need to know our priorities. God has promised that "all these things" will be added to us if we seek Him first. Our tendency is to seek "all these things" and then add God later, if at all.

Sometimes we find our purpose because we know what we do well. In those cases, however, we may well become identified by what we do. When what we do is challenged or taken away, we are devastated. If however, we focus on God first and who we are in Him, our security can never be removed. Even when Job lost his ten children, his wealth, his health, and the respect of his wife, the Bible says he fell down and worshipped!

> And he said, 'Naked I came from my mother's womb, and naked I shall return there. The Lord gave and the Lord has taken away. Blessed be the name of the Lord.'

Through all this Job did not sin nor did he blame God"
(Job 1:21–22).

Second, analyze your temperament. Try to examine what
makes you tick. Examine what your preferences are and what you
enjoy. Determine how you are refueled emotionally and mentally.
Acknowledge your strengths and weaknesses—we all have both.
Perhaps taking the temperament test can be a fun way to see things
that you did not see before. Know yourself. John Calvin reminds us
that, "There is no deep knowing of God without a deep knowing of
self and no deep knowing of self without a deep knowing of God"
(Calvin 1995, 15).

Third, pray. Ask God to show Himself to you as He has revealed
Himself in Jesus Christ. Ask Jesus to forgive you of your sins and
of your rebellion, and surrender your life to Him. Then ask Him to
reveal His purpose for you. Ask God to equip you with what you need
to fulfill His calling for your life. Ask to be called. This may seem a
simple thing, but you would be surprised at how many people, even
Christians, do not ask God for help and direction. He has a plan and
desires to share it with you. Be patient—it will come.

Fourth, share your dreams and concerns with others you can trust
and who believe in you. Align yourself with others who encourage
you, who share your dream, who recognize your calling, and who
appreciate your gifts. God can use other people to help you be
successful and find your purpose. Such important people may tell
us no, or wait, or provide correction which can be important and
necessary in our journey. However, there are also "dream busters"—
people who are threatened by you and are not willing to provide you
with opportunities. They will hinder your purpose and often use you
for their own benefit. Move away from them and stay away.

Fifth, explore possibilities. Sometimes you need to experiment with areas of your calling to see specific aspects emerge. Taking calculated risks allows you to stretch your wings and learn how to fly. Sometimes your purpose requires you to complete additional education and to develop mentoring relationships. You may have to ask someone who believes in you and who has similar gifts to mentor and coach you as you develop your calling.

Sixth, be faithful in little things and watch for open doors. Your purpose may take time to develop. You need to be faithful in little things before you can be faithful in much. Jesus was clear about this concept. In Matthew 25:29. He says, "For to everyone who has, more shall be given." Work with what you have, grow into experiences, and watch what opportunities open as you remain faithful.

In a famous scene from the 1984 movie *Karate Kid*, Daniel (played by Ralph Macchio) becomes confused and discouraged. He has asked Mr. Miyagi (Noriyuki "Pat" Morita) to teach him karate, but the old man has told him to clean cars instead. Daniel doesn't see the (wax on, wax off) hand motions involved in waxing a car as being important. He doesn't make the connection that this is a small but important part of his desired training.

Often, the things we may experience or may be asked to do seem unrelated to our larger goals, and we believe they are a waste of time. However, God may have a purpose leading to His intentions for our lives. Everything we do in life and everything that happens to us is for a larger purpose. We must be faithful and patient and recognize that God is at work in every aspect of our lives. Proverbs 3:6 says, "In all your ways acknowledge Him, and he will make your paths straight." When we aknowledge God in the circumstances of our past we can often see that He had been guiding and preparing us all along for what is taking place in our life now, or for what may lie ahead.

For further study and analysis, go to timlahaye.com. There you will find a more detailed resource and a temperament test that links your temperament with spiritual gifts, ways to serve the church, and ways to serve the marketplace, and offers a further analysis of your strengths and weaknesses. In the meantime, I have provided a brief temperament test in the appendix for your use.* Be aware that it is quite basic and may provide just a start to discovering your temperament and how it may help in on the journey toward knowing your purpose.

There are spiritual-gift assessments available as well. One popular resource is the Network Ministries International materials by Bruce Bugbee and Don Cousins. I encourage you to check them out to gain further insight and direction.

Finally, anticipate the future with peace and confidence. Your purpose is in God's hands. Your life is not your own. You were created and then bought with a precious price indeed—the blood of Jesus Christ. The Lord created you and then redeemed you, so you can be pretty sure that He saved you not just *from* something but *for* something!

---

*   Used by permission - as per Linda LaHaye Murphy.

CHAPTER 9

Discovering and Restoring Purpose

> What you are is God's gift to you; what you become is your gift to God.
>
> —Hans Urs von Balthasar

> This is what the Lord says—your Redeemer, the Holy One of Israel: "I am the Lord your God, who teaches you what is best for you, who directs you in the way you should go."
>
> —Isa. 48:17 NIV

> As obedient children, do not be conformed to the former lusts which were yours in your ignorance, but like the Holy One who called you, be holy yourselves also in all your behavior; because it is written, "You shall be holy, for I am holy."
>
> —1 Peter 1:14–16

Can you identify your passion? Are you beginning to feel a sense of purpose in your life? Does it relate to the betterment of others or is it self-serving? If the latter, God needs to do some adjustments in your life and your vision. Your attitude and your obedience are crucial to the discovery of your purpose. Isaiah

1:19–20 NIV says, "If you are willing and obedient you will eat the best of the land; but if you resist and rebel, you will be devoured by the sword." Again, if you follow God's purpose, you will overcome the world. If you resist Him and rebel, the world will overcome you.

As you consider God's purpose for you based on His word and His blueprint, you may wonder how living a life like that can be even possible. The truth is, it is not possible by simply trying to live the law. No man can do that and be completely successful. That lifestyle is called legalism, where we live our life as if our salvation depends on us. The grace of God through Jesus' finished work frees us from the burden of trying to live by the law. Trying to fulfill God's purpose in our life by our own strength will always have us falling short.

The alternative is to walk in the grace of God, that removes any burden of trying to measure up and find our own way. While grace covers us in all things, we are not called to live a life that simply is filled with sin with the mindset that grace will sanction such a life. The grace through Jesus actually infuses us with the desire to live freely and be moved by His Spirit. Let go and let God is a popular cliché that is often spoken with this truth in mind. The power of the Spirit when we follow Him, leads us to the life that God desires for us, and will empower us to reflect Him. Without the Spirit of God, we are left to simply live the rules as if they were a check list – a very burdensome lifestyle indeed.

To be free to live our purpose, we need to be free to live our purpose. That cannot be done without the grace of God through Jesus. Paul declares:

> There is therefore no condemnation for those who are in Christ Jesus. For the law of the Spirit of life in Christ Jesus has set you free from the law of sin and death. For what the law could not do, weak as it was through the flesh,

> God did: sending His own Son in the likeness of sinful flesh and as an offering for sin, He condemned sin in the flesh, in order that the requirement of the Law might be fulfilled in us, who do not walk according to the flesh, but according to the Spirit. For the mind set on the flesh is death, *but the mind set on the Spirit is life and peace,* because the mind set on the flesh is hostile toward God; for it does not subject itself to the law of God, for it is not even able to do so, *and those who are in the flesh cannot please God* (emphasis mine) (Romans 8:1-8).

Surrender to Christ will free us to fulfill our purpose. The grace of God through Christ will empower us live a life that is free to please God. Our desires will be His, and His desires will be ours. What He feels, we will feel; what he knows we will know. The Spirit of God within us makes it possible to find our way. This is true conversion and transformation. Ask Jesus to rule your life and desires and His Spirit will renew, redirect, and restore your dreams and desires.

Pay attention to your emotions. What makes you angry? What are your "pet peeves?" How do you hurt when others are hurting? What motivates you to "rise to the occasion"? Often such emotions can be a hint as to your passion and calling. These emotions can be a catalyst for you to develop a plan to make a difference in areas of need. Also, are you harboring bitterness and unforgiveness? Do you have a victim mentality? These are just some things that will hinder or even prevent your purpose from emerging.

While I have mentioned some practical considerations in this book, I am not advocating self-help—I am encouraging God-help. Bugbee says:

> The biblical view of God is described in Scripture as creating all things and all people. He is a loving, relational, and intentional God. He is the one who thoughtfully designed you and me to fulfill a meaningful purpose that

will ultimately glorify Him and edify others. If we will listen to His voice, He will give us His perspective of who He is and of who we are to be (Bugbee 1995, 25).

We may often sense our purpose, but internal and external forces might drown out the awareness. In our day and age, we may simply need to slow down, shut off the "noise" in our head or outside stimuli, and contemplate.

Our passion may be hidden, but it has not disappeared! The still, small voice of God speaking to our inner being may be drowned out by the loud business of our lives. We may be living out our purpose before a choice or two we make along the way hinders or destroys our focus, our effectiveness, and our witness. Disappointment and depression may set in. Depression is often a symptom of a repressed purpose. Anxiety can be a fear of not experiencing a fulfilled life. We must stay the course with Christ and not compromise His standards. It is essential for our purpose that we live by God's blueprint. Jesus asked, "And why do you call Me 'Lord, Lord,' and do not do what I say?"(Luke 6:46).

The Devil uses many weapons to misdirect or prevent our purpose. We may not have to find our purpose but rather have our purpose confirmed. We can do this first and foremost by coming to know Jesus Christ, surrendering to Him, and worshipping Him. Paul declares:

> I urge you therefore brethren, by the mercies of God, to present your bodies as a living and holy sacrifice, acceptable to God, which is your spiritual service of worship. And do not be conformed to this world, but be transformed by the renewing of your mind, that you may *prove* what the will of God is, that which is good and acceptable and perfect" (Rom. 12:1–2, emphasis mine).

Paul is suggesting that we simply need to prove the will of God in our lives, indicating that our purpose may not necessarily be that difficult to discover. Whom we worship is an essential choice, as we discovered in chapter 2. Knowing Christ will help us prove our purpose—to ourselves and to others.

We must dream with God. A dream may be our calling. Our destiny in God may emerge through a passion or a dream. As 1 Corinthians 2:9 says, "Things which eye has not seen and ear has not heard, and which have entered the heart of man, all that God has prepared for those who love Him." We should get to know God if we want to see our dreams in more detail. He uses our trials to prepare us for a greater purpose.

There are two paths that can make a difference in fulfilling our purpose. We can either develop a prideful confidence that may turn into brokenness. Or we can develop a humble dependence that can turn into holy confidence. Walker states that "I will never find peace or joy in unholy, unrighteous behaviors" and that "grace and obedience are inseparable" (Walker 2010, 103). The difference is surrendering to God as early as possible in the process of life discovery.

We can know our purpose, but sin, self-centeredness, disobedience, rebellion, and Satan's weapons can wreak havoc upon what has been breathed into our lives and placed upon our spirits. If we align ourselves with the ways of Christ, we may see our purpose emerge. Romans 14:17 says, "The kingdom of God is … righteousness and peace and joy in the Holy Spirit."

We all experience pain and suffering that can douse our sense of purpose. The evil that we choose, or the evil that comes against us, can indeed throw us off the proper path. "Because we cannot live without a sense that our lives make sense, and suffering threatens that confidence, we must find a way to recover, rescue or rehabilitate it" (Rice 2014, 39).

No matter what has occurred in our lives, God can redeem us and bring forth His purpose in us. There is nothing that He cannot overcome, heal, or restore. God empowers us and redeems us. Even when we fall short in trying to follow Christ, God makes forgiveness and restoration available through the blood of Jesus. God's blueprint is for our benefit, and it behooves us to follow His ways. But the good news is that when we fall short, Christ has provided a way of restoration to the Father. We can still experience a purpose-full life.

The Old Testament story of Samson, found in Judges 13–16, is an encouraging portrayal of the redemption of purpose. Samson's mother was barren, but God prophesied to her that she would have a son who would deliver the people of Israel from the evil, slave-making Philistines (Judg. 13:3–5). Samson was the promised son, and his purpose was clear. However, Samson was an insecure, self-centered womanizer. Against his parents' wishes, he desired a Philistine woman to be his wife (Judg. 14:1–3). Despite Samson's stubbornness and rebellion, God used the marriage to allow Samson access to the Philistines, and he was able to slaughter a great number of them. However, it cost the life of his wife and her father (Judg. 15:6).

He then pursued a harlot (Judg. 16:1) and later was duped by Delilah (Judg. 16:15–19), who gave away the secret of his great strength to the conniving Philistines. The Philistines overpowered Samson, gouged out his eyes, and threw him in prison in chains (Judg. 16:21). Samson, called out to God, repented, and had his purpose restored. His strength returned one last time, and he destroyed about three thousand Philistine leaders when he caused a structure in which they were sitting to collapse upon them—and himself. "So the dead whom he killed at his death were more than those he killed in his life" (Judg. 16:30). Samson's purpose as a deliverer of his people was fulfilled despite his sin, rebellion, and weakness. The key for Samson was humbly calling out to God for forgiveness and restoration.

As a Christian counselor and minister, I have found that depression and anxiety are often linked to a lack of purpose. Here is a written example from a client I knew:

> Things like growing up mostly living with my grandmother and not having my single mother around every day began to affect me. In middle school the effects of not having a close relationship with my mother or father started to confuse me. I was depressed about who I was becoming and what type of an adult I would become. If I had to suggest a specific time where I began to get past my confusion and try to establish my identity, it would around 11th grade. I decided to suppress my feelings and regain focus on school. I was expected to go to college, so that's what I did. Not knowing exactly what I wanted a career in, I lost interest in college and dropped out the first semester. Again I was without a plan. When I started working and getting to know God more, I searched myself and forgave myself. Throughout my life's journey I have questioned my purpose. With God, experiences and forgiveness I now know who I am and why I am here. It was not until my late twenties that I can say with a clear conscience that I am who God says I am.

This individual struggled with depression and confusion, clouding the purpose for her life. Once she accepted Christ and began a relationship with God, her life changed. As is often the case, she experienced self-forgiveness for bad decisions and expressed forgiveness to others. As a result, the chains that held her life in confusion and depression were broken and she was released to see her purpose emerge.

Howden and Westgate present four components to spiritual wellness: meaning and purpose in life, inner resources, transcendence, and positive interconnectedness (Howden and Westgate 2006, 5–20). Young people in particular experiment and take risks to find themselves and their purpose. Depression is a major issue as one in five young people have been diagnosed with it (Howden and Westgate 2006, 5–20).

We try to find meaning in life through relationships, sports teams, the arts, substance abuse, vocations, and body image, just to name a few avenues. When we are not sure why we are here, discouragement, depression, and anxiety can occur. But are we looking for our purpose in everything but God? I would say, yes, without a doubt! Our purpose in life has been the focus of this book. (Positive interconnectedness, or a sense of belonging, will be the focus of *Created for Belonging*.)

So what kind of purposeful life did God promise us? Jesus spoke about our purpose while He ministered on earth. On the surface it may seem that Jesus was speaking with a forked tongue. First, He said that He came to give us life and to give it more abundantly (John 10:10). Abundant life is not simply what we will experience when we reach paradise. Abundant life includes "copious amounts of fruitfulness, lavish amounts of love, abundant supplies of strength and courage, and profuse amounts of generosity" (Larson 2013, 20). We can experience these things through the gracious hand of God, through the lives of many around us, through a generous attitude, and as a result of living according to His ways.

On the other hand, Jesus warned us that life here on earth would also include hardships, hurts, disappointments, and tribulations (John 16:33). So which is it? Can we pursue our purpose in God and experience abundant life in a world where forces come against us?

Yes! But because we face these forces, it is critical that we submit to the Lord and follow after Him.

> For what credit is there if, when you sin and are harshly treated, you endure it with patience? But if when you do what is right and suffer for it you patiently endure it, this finds favor with God. For you have been called for this purpose, since Christ also suffered for you, leaving you an example for you to follow in His steps, who committed no sin, nor was any deceit found in His mouth; and while being reviled, He did not revile in return; while suffering, He uttered no threats, but kept entrusting Himself to Him who judges righteously. (1 Peter 2:20–23)

The enemy of our soul is seeking to turn us against God and to destroy us. As we saw in chapter 7, the Devil uses his weapons to prevent us from seeking God, from serving Him, and from finding our true purpose. He will oppose us and try to render us ineffective through life's circumstances.

When we experience hurts in relationships, we often feel discouraged from our purpose. One of my previous students wrote:

> I think He has big plans for us all; it is just up to us to listen to Him and follow the path He has chosen for us to follow. I have struggled over the past 13 years to get back to school and to really find myself. It doesn't help when you are in relationship with someone who does not encourage your potential. However, I finally feel like I know who I am and where I want to be in life. Sometimes, no matter how bad the hurt, we have to let go of the things or people who hold us back from reaching our full potential.

This person's purpose was hampered by not knowing who she was, by not having someone who would share her vision, and by not experiencing a safe and loving relationship. Notice how our core longings are intertwined with one another and how we need to have God meet those longings in all areas. He intends to turn bad into good, unknown into known, no purpose into purpose, lack of safety into safety, misunderstanding into understanding, unloved into loved, and loneliness and rejection into belonging. This is the essence of redemption!

The forces of evil are warring against the Spirit of God for the hearts of human beings. The church is under attack. The family is under attack. Righteousness is being watered down at a rapid pace. Our purpose is at stake. Larson says, "Satan came to steal it from us, to kill our dreams and our passion, and destroy every hint of God-inspired sparkle and verse within us (See John 10:10)" (Larson 2013, 20). It is time to return to what works—God's blueprint. It is time to shed the "sloppy agape," "anything goes" message of the current culture and church. Grace may be free to us, but it cost God everything! While grace is indeed available to all of us through Christ, Paul says emphatically, "What shall we say then? Are we to continue in sin that grace might increase? *May it never be*! How shall we who died to sin still live in it?" (Rom. 6:1–2, emphasis mine). Tolerance at all costs, is not a fruit of the Spirit. It is an idol of our time. It is time to stop compromising and stay true to our calling.

The Devil will use his weapons to immobilize and even destroy us. If he is successful, then we become less than what we were meant to be. We may become more hurtful than helpful. We may bring more death than life. We may reflect the author of death instead of the author of life. Rice says, "Moreover, the view that evil is a corruption of the good also reminds us that the greater someone's capacity for good is, the greater the evil of which he or she is capable" (Rice 2014, 54). Because we have been created with such a great capacity for good or evil, we need to be anchored to the truth—the person of Jesus Christ. As created, reflective beings, we will reflect something or someone! That is what is at stake—reflecting death or life. Remember that we mirror what we value, pursue, and worship.

Here is what one of my students wrote about her role as a wife, a mother, a home-school teacher, and a student herself.

> My place of work matters. I know it matters to God because He has asked that everything I do, I do unto Him. As of late, it has been hard ... very hard to focus on my schoolwork. I take it personally because it isn't "just" school. I have given glory to God for all academic achievements since entering school. One would wonder, how could sitting in front of a computer doing work qualify for a job that matters to God? It matters if it brings glory to His name. What happens, though, when we don't do our best? When we get distracted? When life comes full force and we still have to perform? We fall into the group of commoners who fail to succeed because of dominating powers in this world. It matters, because as a Christian, what we do, in some form or fashion, benefits someone else. It either serves as motivation or as a gentle rebuke to those who could do more and don't. The attitude I display at home in what I do, and how I do it, will serve as a model to others the moment I step out to another field of work that matters to God. When I am able to give my work the value it deserves in the hands of God, I trigger a change in events in my performance, in my product, and in the lives of those I serve. It matters, because I have moved passed the self-involved world of youth into the realistic world of servanthood ... where we all serve—some joyfully, others under obligations. But at the end of the day, realizing what matters to God helps form the mold of what it is that needs to matter to me.

What a powerful, insightful declaration! Her attitude shows a refreshing integrity. The dominating powers in this world that she mentions are apathy, entitlement, selfishness, evil ambition, rebellion, dishonor, power grabbing, and laziness. Add to those the weapons of Satan, and it is clear that we need Jesus to restore our purpose and the work ethic needed to fulfill that purpose.

When our purpose is tied to self-glory, God often has a way of redirecting our paths. In Matthew 19:16–26, Jesus addresses a rich young ruler. The man claimed to have kept all of the commandments that Jesus listed in the conversation. Then Jesus asked him to sell all his possessions, give to the poor, and come follow Him. The man could not do it and went away grieved. He could not give up his self-created identity. As a result, he could not experience the purpose God had for him. "People with wrong values are obsessed with stockpiling symbols: a luxury car, a job title, exotic, vacations. Their life's goal is to possess the appropriate *chic* icons by which to measure their worth" (original emphasis)(Walker 2000, 58). As 1 John 2:15 says, "Do not love the world, nor the things in the world. If anyone loves the world, the love of the Father is not in him."

In the 2004 movie *Troy*, which depicts a story from Greek mythology, Achilles (played by Brad Pitt) tries to decide whether he should go to war against the city of Troy. He knows he is the most feared and respected warrior in the world. And he has enjoyed great glory. When Achilles seeks his mother's advice about entering what would become an epic war between the Greeks and the Trojans, she declares, "Your glory walks hand in hand with your doom." What a powerful line! That is true for all of us. If we seek glory, it will lead to our doom. Are we seeking glory or are we pursuing our purpose to glorify God?

Humanity's entire purpose hinges on these first commandments. "And the one who keeps His commandments abides in Him, and He in him. And we know by this that He abides in us, by the Spirit whom He has given us" (1 John 3:24). Are we pleasing God or are we pleasing ourselves? The discovery of our purpose hinges upon the answer to that question!

Pursuing our purpose takes discipline. Many people are disciplined in areas of diet, exercise, study habits, and work ethic. However, discipline is a lifestyle—one that is not as widespread as it should be. Discipline requires restraint, patience, and self-denial. We need to say no to sin, temptation, unrighteous compromise, and self-centered justifications. Saying no takes discipline. The result of discipline is godliness and the discovery of our purpose. "Discipline yourself for the purpose of godliness … godliness is profitable for all things, since it holds promise for the present life and also for the life to come" (1 Tim. 4:7–8).

The Lord Jesus Christ made it clear to all who would listen how He saw His own purpose. Jesus said, "I can do nothing on My own initiative. As I hear, I judge; and My judgment is just, because I do not seek my own will, but the will of Him who sent me" (John 5:30). Forty-seven times in the gospel of John, Jesus declares that He is doing His Father's will. The more he sought His Father, the more He knew the Father's purpose.

In John 8:28–29 Jesus says:

> When you lift up the Son of Man, then you will know that I am He, and I do nothing on my own initiative, but I speak these things as the Father taught Me. And He who sent Me is with Me; He has not left Me alone, for I always do the things that are pleasing to Him.

Oh, to have the attitude of Christ. Oh, to see the rewards of such an attitude. God desires that for all of us. "The Lord will guide you always; he will satisfy your needs in a sun-scorched land and will strengthen your frame. You will be like a well-watered garden, like a spring whose waters never fail" (Isa. 58:11 NIV).

Even though John the Baptist had a prominent role in preparing the way for the Messiah and introducing Him to the world, he made a statement that we could all adopt as a motto if we want to know our purpose: "He must increase, but I must decrease" (John 3:30). One of my students wrote:

> God transformed my plans and my dreams. I used to want to dance on Broadway—to see my name in lights—but I wanted more. I wanted purpose in my life. He gave me purpose. He transformed my life. Before I surrendered to God's will for my life, I was nothing. My life had no purpose or meaning. Today, I have the privilege of serving my God. This life is not my own. I am above no job. It is a privilege to be alive, and it is only by the grace of God that I am alive.

The things of the Spirit can rarely be reduced to formulas. However, allow me to provide one that is loose enough to describe the power of the gospel and the finished work of Christ. Our purpose begins with giving our lives to Jesus and asking Him to be our Savior and Lord. Doing so restores us to relationship with God, the author and purpose-giver of our lives. Then His Holy Spirit begins to transform us to become more like Jesus. He is manifested in our lives by the fruit of the spirit. "But the fruit of the Spirit is love, joy, peace, patience, kindness, goodness, faithfulness, gentleness, self-control; against such things there is no law" (Gal. 5:22–23). We are admonished in 1 Peter 2:15–16:

> For such is the will of God that by doing right you may silence the ignorance of foolish men. Act as free men, and

do not use your freedom as a covering for evil but use it as
bondslaves of God.

How true it is that no laws speak against the fruit of the Spirit.

As we live by the fruit of the Spirit, we gain the ability to live the
law. The fruit of the Spirit possesses "being" qualities, and the gifts
of the Spirit have "doing" qualities. The fruit of the Spirit comes by
our surrender to and walk with Christ; the gifts of the Spirit are given
as endowments by God to be a blessing to others in the world and in
His kingdom (Bugbee 1995, 65). We are not capable of living the law
in our flesh and without the Spirit of God within us. If our lives do
not show godly fruit, then we must ask if we have been transformed
by Jesus.

Our salvation for eternity is a gracious gift given by a loving God
through the life, death, and resurrection of His Son. Jesus said, "This
is the work of God, that you believe in Him who he has sent" (John
6:29). That work begins our purpose in life. Our work is to surrender
our lives to Christ. As we surrender to Jesus, He provides His Holy
Spirit to work within us to produce fruit and the power to live the
law and to live our purpose. We walk in His grace which empowers
to live according to God's blueprint.

The formula: **Jesus** in our lives = **Fruit** growing from
our lives = **Power** to live life with purpose

Our purpose on earth:

- To love and worship God Almighty through Jesus Christ.
- To accept the grace of God and *His* righteousness for our
  lives.

- To reflect and glorify God in what we do, no matter where we do it.
- To follow God's ways and keep His commandments.
- To suffer and be ridiculed for righteousness' sake.
- To be leaders in many capacities, in various ways, in whatever arena we serve.
- To die to pride and arrogance, and serve others
- To seek the good of others, especially those we love.
- To live and work with integrity.
- To be good stewards.
- To be devoted to family, to spouse, to our call, to God.
- To be faithful to those we love, with what we have, and in what we do. When we are, we will see growth.
- To show mercy and to be considerate of others.
- To be life-givers.
- To love and protect life.
- To be content and therefore experience peace.
- To give and to be generous and gracious.
- To be loved by God!

We can be confident that God has a specific purpose for each of us stemming from these general purposes and depending upon our personality, temperament, passions, calling, and gifts. God loves us and wants to communicate what He desires for us. It will be good for us and for others as well. Psalm 1:1-3 should encourage us:

> How blessed is the man who does not walk in the counsel of the wicked, nor stand in the path of sinners, nor sit in the seat of scoffers! But his delight is in the law of the Lord, and in His law he meditates day and night. And he will be like a tree firmly planted by streams of water,

which yields its fruit in its season, and its leaf does not wither; and in whatever he does, he prospers.

Our purpose can be found:

- By surrendering our lives to Jesus Christ and recognizing that our identities are found in Him.
- By loving and worshipping God. When we do this, we will want to follow Him and His ways.
- By slowing down to listen to God and to our own spirits.
- By reading His Word, the Bible.
- By being in dialogue with God through prayer and personal reflection, listening to the Holy Spirit.
- By discovering our passions. Each of us has at least one.
- By discovering and using our gifts. Each of us has something to offer.
- By seeking the common good and well-being of others.
- By seeking forgiveness and extending it to others.
- By learning to be content—seeking peace, not just happiness.
- By overcoming the weapons of Satan with truth, knowing that God loves us and wants the best for us.
- By seeking grace and healing through our suffering and disappointments.
- By seeking out people who bring out the best in us and who admonish, correct, and encourage us in our pursuit of God and our purpose.
- By waiting on God and trusting Him.
- By being holy.

When we know we are loved, we will be more creative, more courageous, and more willing to pursue our dream and our calling.

Because God loves us, He provides a blueprint for life that includes the way of freedom through obedience to His commands. The love of God encourages us to be who we were meant to be. Ezekiel 36:26-27 states:

> Moreover, I will give you a new heart and put a new spirit within you; and I will remove the heart of stone from your flesh and give you a heart of flesh. And *I will put my Spirit within you* and *cause you to walk* in My statutes, and you will be careful to observe My ordinances. (emphasis mine)

God empowers us to live our purpose. If we believe that God is out to get us or to withhold His love from us, then we will doubt and hold back, preventing us from receiving from God, being blessed, and being a blessing to others.

I would like to end with words from the Lord to all who have come this far. The first was initially spoken to Joshua, who was about to transition from following Moses to being the next leader of the people of Israel. God groomed him, loved him, promised to be with him, and launched him into his calling. Let these words encourage you.

> Only be strong and very courageous; be careful to do according to all the law which Moses my servant commanded you; do not turn from it to the right or to the left, so that you may *have success wherever you go.* This book of the law shall not depart from your mouth, but you shall meditate on it day and night, so that you may be careful to do according to all that is written in it; *for then you will make your way prosperous, and then you will have success.* (Josh. 1:7–8, emphasis mine)

The second word is from the apostle Peter—a man who came to know his purpose through much confusion, disappointment, and surrender.

> To sum up, let all be *harmonious, sympathetic, brotherly, kindhearted, and humble in spirit*; not returning evil for evil, or insult for insult, but giving a blessing instead; for you were *called for the very purpose that you might inherit a blessing*. For, let him who means to love life and see good days *refrain his tongue from evil* and his lips from speaking guile. And let him *turn away from evil and do good*; let him *seek peace and pursue it*. For the eyes of the Lord are upon the righteous and His ears attend to their prayer, but the face of the Lord is against those who do evil. (1 Peter 3:8–12, emphasis mine)

May you find your purpose and the power to fulfill it through the love of Jesus in your life!

APPENDIX
Temperament Test

T he charts below represent strengths and weaknesses for each of the four temperaments. Please keep in mind that we all have strengths and weaknesses, so the more honest you are as you complete this assessment, the more accurate your scores will be. Once you complete each column, follow these directions to obtain your score.

- Add up the totals for each column under each of the four sections.

- Add the totals from the strengths and the weaknesses under each section and divide by two.

- Each section will then have one total.

- Enter the total for each section (I, II, III, IV) that corresponds to the section number on the last page. (The section number has the specific temperament.) That total represents your primary temperament.

- Your primary temperament will usually be in the 40 to 70 range, and your secondary temperament will usually be in the 20 to 50 range.

- Once you obtain your score, return to chapter 8 and match your score with potential vocations. Have fun with this exercise, and remember that this is just a guide for personal discovery. The Lord Jesus still has your ultimate plan and purpose.

I.

Strengths		**Weaknesses**	
Outgoing	_____	Loud	_____
Charismatic	_____	Egocentric	_____
Compassionate	_____	Exaggerates	_____
Friendly	_____	Fearful & Insecure	_____
Responsive	_____	Undisciplined	_____
Enthusiastic	_____	Weak-Willed	_____
Talkative	_____	Restless	_____
Carefree	_____	Disorganized	_____
Generous	_____	Unproductive	_____
Warm/Approachable	_____	Undependable	_____
Total	_____	Total	_____

Least like me: 0–3. Somewhat like me: 4–6. A lot like me: 7–10.

II.

Strengths		Weaknesses	
Determined &		Proud	_____
Strong-Willed	_____	Crafty & Sly	_____
Independent	_____	Hostile-Angry	_____
Self-Confident	_____	Cruel-Sarcastic	_____
Productive	_____	Cold-Unsympathetic	_____
Visionary	_____	Insensitive &	
Optimistic	_____	Inconsiderate	_____
Courageous	_____	Opinionated &	
Practical	_____	Prejudiced	_____
Decisive	_____	Self-Sufficient	_____
Leader	_____	Unforgiving	_____
		Domineering	_____

Total _____   Total _____

Least like me: 0–3. Somewhat like me: 4–6. A lot like me: 7–10.

III.

Strengths		Weaknesses	
Gifted	————	Moody	————
Loyal	————	Negative	————
Sensitive	————	Critical	————
Analytical	————	Touchy	————
Idealistic	————	Self-Centered	————
Perfectionist	————	Rigid & Legalistic	————
Conscientious	————	Vengeful	————
Self-Sacrificing	————	Persecution-Prone	————
Artistic	————	Unsociable	————
Self-Disciplined	————	Theoretical and Often Impractical	————
Total	———————	Total	———————

Least like me: 0–3. Somewhat like me: 4–6. A lot like me: 7–10.

IV.

Strengths		Weaknesses	
Calm	————	Unmotivated	————
Quiet	————	Blasé	————
Practical	————	Procrastinator	————
Easygoing	————	Spectator	————
Likeable	————	Selfish	————
Diplomatic	————	Stingy	————
Efficient	————	Stubborn	————
Dependable	————	Self-protective	————
Organized	————	Indecisive	————
Conservative	————	Fearful	————
Dry Humor	————		

Total ——————   Total ——————

Least like me: 0–3. Somewhat like me: 4–6. A lot like me: 7–10.

I.   Sanguine   -   Score: ——————
II. Choleric   -   Score: ——————
III. Melancholy   -   Score: ——————
IV. Phlegmatic   -   Score: ——————

References

http://www.fbi.gov/news/pressrel/press-releases/fbi-releases-2012-crime-statistics. Retrieved March 25, 2014.

http://www.myaddiction.com/education/articles/sex_statistics.html. 2013. Retrieved March 24, 2014.

http://www.rawstory.com/rs/2013/09/16/u-s-murder-rate-higher-than-nearly-all-other-developed-countries-fbi-data; Agence France-Presse, September 16, 2013. Retrieved March 11, 2014.

http://www.goodtherapy.org/blog/holding-grudge-bad-for-health-0410122. 2012. Retrieved August 1, 2014.

https://www.ligonier.org/learn/articles/sabbath-rest/

American Heritage Dictionary of the English Language. 4th ed. 2006. Boston, MA: Houghton Mifflin Company.

Anderson, Neil. 2000. *The Bondage Breaker.* Harvest House Publishing. Eugene, OR.

Archer, Gleason L., R. Laird Harris, and Bruce K. Waltke. 1980. *Theological Wordbook of the Old Testament.* Vol. I. Chicago, IL: Moody Press.

Barnett, Matthew. 2011. *The Cause within You.* Carol Stream, IL: BarnaBooks.

Barry, Michael. 2011. *The Forgiveness Project: The Startling Discovery of How to Overcome Cancer, Find Health, and Achieve Peace.* Grand Rapids, MI: Kregel Publishers.

Beale, G. K. 2008. *We Become What We Worship.* Downer Grove, IL: InterVarsity Press.

Berger, Kathleen Stassen. 2011. *The Developing Person through the Life Span.* 8th ed. New York, NY: Worth Publishers.

Boyd, Gregory A. 2004. *Repenting of Religion.* Grand Rapids, MI: Baker Books.

Briscoe, Stuart. 1991. *Hearing God's Voice above the Noise*. Wheaton, IL: Victor Books.

Bugbee, Bruce. 1995. *What You Do Best in the Body of Christ*. Grand Rapids, MI: Zondervan.

Calvin, John. 1995. *Institutes of the Christian Religion*. 1536 ed. Trans. Ford Lewis Battle. Grand Rapids, MI: Eerdmans, 15. Quoted in David Benner, *The Gift of Being Yourself* (Downers Grove, IL: InterVarsity Press, 2004).

Comfort, Ray. 1989. *Hell's Best Kept Secret*. Springdale, PA: Whitaker House Publishers.

Fowler, J. W. 1995. *Stages of Faith: The Psychology of Human Development and the Quest for Healing*. New York, NY: HarperOne.

Frankl, Viktor Emil. 2006. *Man's Search for Meaning*. New York, NY: Beacon Press.

Frangipane, Francis. 2006. *The Three Battlegrounds*. Cedar Rapids, IA: Arrow Publications, Inc.

Galloway, Stephen. 2015. *Jennifer is Just Fine*. The Hollywood Reporter. January 30, 2015.

Gentile, Douglas A. 2003. *Media Violence and Children*. Westport, CT: Praeger.

Hall, Laurie. 1996. *An Affair of the Mind*. Wheaton, IL: Tyndale House Publishers.

Harris, R. Laird, Archer, Gleason L., Waltke, Bruce K. 1980. *Theological Wordbook of the Old Testament*. Vol. I. Moody Press. Chicago, IL.

Heffernan, Virginia. Yahoo! News Coorespondent. *Neil Armstrong, The Moon's Mystery Man*. Yahoo! News/The Lookout. Accessed August 26, 2012.

Holy Bible, New Living Translation. 1996. Wheaton, IL: Tyndale House Publishing.

Howden, J. W. and C. E. Westgate. 2006. "Spiritual Wellness and Depression: Testing a Theoretical Model with Older Adolescents and Midlife Adults." *Counseling & Values* 51(1): 5–20.

Idleman, Kyle. 2013. *Gods at War*. Grand Rapids, MI: Zondervan Publishers.

Institute of Medicine. 2006. *Sleep Disorders and Sleep Deprivation: An Unmet Public Health Problem*. Washington, D.C: The National Academies Press.

Jennings, Tim. 2013. *The God-Shaped Brain*. Downer Grove, IL: InterVarsity Press.

Laaser, Mark and Debra. 2008. *The Seven Desires of Every Heart*. Grand Rapids, MI: Zondervan Publishers.

LaHaye, Tim. 1991. *Transforming Your Temperament*. Wheaton, IL: Tyndale House Publishers.

Larson, Susie. 2013. *Your Beautiful Purpose*. Minneapolis, MN: Bethany House Publishers.

Master Study Bible, New American Standard Version. 1981. Nashville, TN: Holman Bible Publishers.

Oxford American College Dictionary, 2002. New York, NY: G. P. Putnam's Sons.

Remig, Anita. 2010. "Childhood Developmental Disorders: Autism, Asperger's, Bipolar, ADHD, Nonverbal Learning Disability, Tourette's and Other Related Disorders." Continuing education lecture conducted by professor and researcher from the University of New Hampshire, Fayetteville, NC, December 3, 2010.

Rice, Richard. 2104. *Suffering and the Search for Meaning: Contemporary Responses to the Problem of Pain*. Downers Grove, IL: IVP Academic, an imprint of Intervarsity Press.

Robertson, Pat. 2004. *The Ten Offenses: Reclaim the Blessings of the Ten Commandments*. Nashville, TN: Integrity Publishers.

Rosenbaum, Philip. 1994. *The Promise*. Nashville, TN: Broadman & Holman Publishers.

Sherman, Doug and William Hendricks. 1987. *Your Work Matters to God*. Colorado Springs, CO: NavPress.

Strong, James. 1981. *Strong's Exhaustive Concordance*. Grand Rapids, MI: Baker Book House.

Treat, Casey. 1999. *Renewing the Mind*. Tulsa, OK: Harrison House Publishers.

Walker, James. 2000. *Husbands Who Won't Lead and Wives Who Won't Follow*. Minneapolis, MN: Bethany House Publishers.

Walker, Jon. 2010. *Costly Grace*. Abilene, TX. Leafwood Publishers.

Wardle, Terry. 2005. *Wounded*. Abilene TX: Leafwood Publishers.

Warren, Rick. 2002. *The Purpose Driven Life*. Grand Rapids, MI: Zondervan Publishing House.

Weirsbe, Warren. 2007. *The Weirsbe Bible Commentary.* Colorado Springs, CO: David C. Cook Publishers.

Webster's New World College Dictionary. 4th ed. 2001. Foster City, CA: IDG Books Worldwide, Inc.

Wright, Alan D. 2005. *Shame Off You: Washing Away the Mud That Hides Our True Selves.* Sisters, OR: Multnomah Publishers.

Yalom, Irvin D. 1980. *Existential Psychotherapy.* New York, NY: BasicBooks.

About the Author

Christian counselor Dr. Robert B. Shaw Jr. is a Licensed Clinical Mental Health Counselor and Supervisor, dually licensed in Virginia and North Carolina. He is also an ordained minister, serving as a youth pastor, Christian education director, adult education director, musician, and executive pastor in churches in New Jersey, Colorado, Maryland, and in North Carolina, for over twenty-five years. He has also been a middle school and high school teacher and athletic coach in both the public and private school environments. Dr. Shaw has spent several years counseling in church settings and community agencies and counseling military personnel and their families near Ft. Bragg, North Carolina. He also ministers regularly in the Philippines. He specializes in trauma related issues; addictions; and victims of abuse, depression, anxiety disorders, life adjustment issues, loss and grief, counseling church leaders and pastors, adolescents, and adults. Dr. Shaw's is a unique prophetic voice in the kingdom caring for hurting people, and he serves as an adjunct professor for a Christian university, an author, and a sought-after conference speaker. Dr. Shaw has a Bachelor of Arts degree in religious studies from Wagner College, New York and a Master of Divinity degree from Christian

International Theological School, Florida. He also has a Master of Arts in professional counseling from Liberty University, Virginia and a Doctor of Ministry degree in formational counseling, a practical theology, from Ashland Theological Seminary, Ohio. He is a member of the American Association of Christian Counseling. Dr. Shaw enjoys running, sports, the beach, and spending time with friends and family.

Printed in the United States
by Baker & Taylor Publisher Services